CO-ASZ-182

GF
13
H57

32676

DATE DUE

North Hennepin
Community College Library
7411 85th Avenue North
Brooklyn Park, MN 55445

HISTORICAL ECOLOGY

CONTRIBUTORS

Edward M. Anson is Associate Professor of History at the University of Arkansas at Little Rock. A graduate of the University of Virginia, he specializes in the history of the Greek and Roman worlds.

Lester J. Bilsky is Associate Professor of History at the University of Arkansas at Little Rock. A graduate of the University of Washington, he is now studying ecological problems and attitudes towards the environment in ancient China. He is the author of *The State Religion of Ancient China* (1975).

Arthur S. Boughey has recently retired as Professor of Human Ecology at the University of California, Irvine. A graduate of the University of Edinburgh, he is the author of such books as *Man and the Environment* (1971), *Ecology of Populations* (1973), and *Strategy for Survival* (1976).

Charles R. Bowlus is Associate Professor of History at the University of Arkansas at Little Rock. A graduate of the University of Massachusetts, his work deals with the economic and military history of Central Europe in medieval times. He has written *Die Ostmark als Karolingische Grenzraum* (forthcoming).

John M. Culbertson is Professor of Economics at the University of Wisconsin. A graduate of the University of Michigan, he is the author of such works as *Full Employment or Stagnation* (1964), *Macroeconomic Theory and Stabilization Policy* (1968), and *Economic Development: An Ecological Approach* (1971).

Thomas F. Glick is Associate Professor of History and Geography at Boston University. A graduate of Harvard University, his work includes *Irrigation and Society in Medieval Valencia* (1970), and *The Old World Background of the Irrigation System of San Antonio, Texas* (1972).

David J. Herlihy is Professor of History at Harvard University. A graduate of Yale University, he is the author of such works as *Pisa in the Early Renaissance* (1957), *Medieval and Renaissance Pistoia* (1967), and *Medieval Culture and Society* (1968).

Michael P. Hoffman is Associate Professor of Anthropology at the University of Arkansas at Fayetteville. A graduate of Harvard University, he has been involved in several archaeological digs and has published articles and monographs on the prehistory of Arkansas and other regions of North America.

J. Donald Hughes is Professor of History at the University of Denver. A graduate of Boston University, he has written such works as *Ecology in Ancient Civilizations* (1975), and "Effect of Classical Cities on the Mediterranean Landscape," in *Ekistics* (1976).

Thomas E. Kaiser is Assistant Professor of History at the University of Arkansas at Little Rock. A graduate of Harvard University, he specializes in the intellectual history of eighteenth and nineteenth century Europe.

Carl H. Moneyhon is Associate Professor of History at the University of Arkansas at Little Rock. A graduate of the University of Chicago, his work is concerned with U.S. government and society in the late nineteenth century. He is the author of *Republicanism in Reconstruction Texas* (1980).

HISTORICAL ECOLOGY

*Essays on Environment
and
Social Change*

Edited by

LESTER J. BILSKY

National University Publications
KENNIKAT PRESS // 1980
Port Washington, N.Y. // London

GF
13
H57

Copyright © 1980 by Kennikat Press Corp. All rights reserved. No part of this publication may be reproduced, stored in a retrieval system, or transmitted, in any form or by any means, electronic, mechanical, photocopying, recording, or otherwise, without the prior written permission of the publisher.

Manufactured in the United States of America

Published by
Kennikat Press Corp.
Port Washington, N.Y. / London

Library of Congress Cataloging in Publication Data
Main entry under title:

Historical ecology.

(National university publications)
First presented as a series of lectures at the University of Arkansas at Little Rock.
Bibliography: p.
Includes index.
1. Human ecology—History—Addresses, essays, lectures. 2. Man—Influence of environment—History—Addresses, essays, lectures. 3. Social change—Addresses, essays, lectures. I. Bilsky, Lester J., 1935-
GF13.H57   301.31   79-19136

Library of Congress Cataloging in Publication Data

ISBN 0-8046-9247-5

32676

Contents

Introduction

by Carl H. Moneyhon

As inhabitants of a modern industrial society, we have become painfully aware that the conditions governing our lives and our social systems are directly related to our environment. The organization of our economic system, technology, politics, and other cultural institutions reflect the nature of existing resources and their availability. However, we do not, as yet, fully understand the precise ways in which society and nature interrelate. We have learned that shifts in resource bases can spark a variety of structural responses in our society, but we do not always know how to interpret what occurs in specific cases, nor can we predict accurately the outcome of our evolving interaction with the environment. We do not even know whether or not social change as a response to modifications in the environment can be controlled, but even if it can be controlled, our general lack of knowledge limits our ability to respond to environmental change.

The contributors to this volume believe that our understanding of current environmental problems can be enhanced through the study of similar problems in the past. Recognizing that earlier societies experienced institutional changes which were tied, in one way or another, to shifting relationships with their environments, we see opportunities to examine case histories of ecological crises in their entirety. By thus gaining the perspectives of time and distance, we may achieve greater objectivity and develop new approaches to the analysis of situations in the past that present numerous parallels to ours in the present.

These essays were first presented as a series of lectures on the history of ecological crises given at the University of Arkansas at Little Rock. Several members of the university's history department who had begun to work on environmental history conceived of the lecture series as a means of comparing a broad range of past ecological crises and of looking for relationships between the events of the past and the current world crisis. The lectures were made possible through the generosity of the Arkansas Humanities Program, the George W. Donaghey Foundation of Little Rock, a few private donors attracted to the series' subject matter, and by several units of the University of Arkansas at Little Rock, its Department of History in particular.

In our endeavor to explore a wide range of scholarly activity in the field of ecological history, we solicited contributions from a variety of scholars engaging in several types of methodology. The eclectic nature of the papers collected here indicates, then, the diversity of the work going on in this field, the relative youth of the discipline, and the lack, at present, of precise disciplinary boundaries.

We have organized the lectures into four major units based upon methodological and chronological criteria. The first unit presents a broad conceptual framework for the examination of historical ecology, focusing on the work of biologists, geographers, and anthropologists and the models they have developed to deal with ecological issues. The next three units are devoted to examinations of specific civilizations and communities that have faced ecological crises: first, two ancient communities that can be characterized as primarily agrarian civilizations; second, the European Middle Ages, when, as historians have begun to appreciate, ecological forces had a profound effect upon cultural development; and, third, efforts made by modern industrialized societies to deal with their ecological problems.

We can suggest that only very limited conclusions be drawn from these essays. To better understand social change in crisis periods, it seems important, first, to understand those elements of a community's social structure directly related to its peculiar environmental relationship and system of resource utilization. Adaptation to the environment may prove difficult should these elements constitute essential parts of a community's identity. In addition, it seems important to locate the mechanisms a society possesses to transform perceptions of the environment and its effects into public policy. In any crisis state, normally numerous solutions are conceivable, there being no one, "correct" mode of dealing with environmental problems. A society might attempt to maintain its basic social structure by attempting to exploit the environment more vigorously. Alternatively, it might choose to reorganize itself, changing some of its institutions—perhaps through a concentration of power—in order to preserve others. Some combination of these responses is also possible.

The nature of a community's action will be conditioned by the ideology informing its behavior. Since an ideology includes a particular set of social values, which, in turn, are predicated on a particular mode of interaction with the society's environment, a change in any part of this mode of interaction might well present a challenge to the continued existence of the society as such. Refusing to change the complex of rules and values of a society will limit its members' capacity to respond to environmental crisis conditions; change, however, opens the door to social and political chaos.

At this point, the message that a study of environmental history brings us is not very optimistic. Nevertheless, if we are to find the best possible solutions to environmental crisis, we must not allow ourselves to be deluded by rosy technocratic visions which do not take into account the realities and demands of social organization. We must, instead, recognize what is feasible, given the nature of our cultural as well as natural environment, by studying the experiences of the past.

PART ONE

HISTORICAL ECOLOGY: FUNDAMENTAL FACTORS

Introduction

by Lester J. Bilsky

The two essays included in this section present an overview of relationships between man and nature, a survey of concepts to orient the reader before he confronts the specific case studies of past environmental problems and attitudes comprising the remainder of this volume. The essays are the work of scholars who deal with man's place in nature in the broadest terms, one a specialist in the field of human ecology and the other an anthropologist.

The former, Professor Boughey, offers a schema for the significant developmental stages of human culture based on advances in man's ability to manipulate the environment. In any stage, if, because of climatic change, exhaustion of resources, population growth, or some combination of these and other such factors, a human society's population exceeds its territory's capacity to support it, that society faces an environmental crisis. If it is not to disintegrate the society must adjust to its problem. Successful adjustments in the past have involved population controls, expansion of living area achieved either through migration to a new frontier or annexation of the territory of others, or new technological capabilities.

Professor Hoffman, who, as an anthropologist, has access to the domain of pre and proto-history, presents several vivid examples of man's problems with his environment and of the consequent effects on populations and modes of behavior. He tells of the late Pleistocene hunters in North America whose lack of adaptation to conditions in a new world may have caused the destruction of their basic food resource. He shows how the Aztecs in a similar situation found a direct, if drastic, way of solving the problem of inadequate diet, while keeping their population under control. He contrasts the failures of Pueblo Indians in the American Southwest and Vikings in Greenland to respond to deteriorating environmental conditions with the success experienced by the inhabitants of the early Near East, where limited resources pushed people to introduce the technological innovations that made agriculture and, ultimately, civilized life possible.

Both authors' work displays the reality of a vital but often overlooked factor in human existence. Man's relationship to his environment is not merely a unidirectional one, whereby he imposes his will upon the natural world; it is, instead, one of mutuality in which human behavior is also profoundly affected by natural forces. Our current ecological crisis is a prime example of the effects of this factor. As Professor Boughey points out, the depletion of natural resources and the pollution we have caused will force us to modify our behavior. Both authors indicate that such modifications will transform modern society, perhaps in ways quite different from our current expectations.

CHAPTER ONE

Environmental Crises—
Past and Present

by A. S. Boughey

There can be no doubt that at the present time, all human societies, whatever their stage of development, are facing one aspect or another of an environmental crisis of major proportions. This may take the form of energy and water shortages, as it does in the United States; it may be in the nature of a permanent scarcity of critical mineral resources, as in Japan and many Western European nations. In certain underdeveloped nations, such as Bangladesh, Ethiopia, and the Sahelian regions of West Africa, there may be an ever present threat of general famine. In some instances, the environmental crisis may have additional and more social dimensions, as for example in the United States, where crimes against persons—robbery, burglary, rape, kidnap, terrorism, and other violent forms of mayhem—have reached proportions unprecedented in an advanced industrial nation.

We are now beginning to perceive that at least some manifestations of this latest environmental crisis are brought about by perturbations of our global climatic systems presently entirely beyond our control. Variations in the energy received from the sun by this planet can apparently cause modifications of the mean ambient global temperatures of as much as one or two degrees, quite sufficient to bring about the onset of a mini-ice age such as occurred in the northern hemisphere in the seventeenth and eighteenth centuries. Such perturbations can also cause variation in the cosmic radiation to which we are subjected and thereby influence the depth of our planet's protective ozone layer and the amount of ultraviolet radiation penetrating to the earth's surface. Additionally, the temperature changes might well influence the direction of the high altitude jet streams that in part control the distribution of rainfall over the surface of the globe. One result in the United States could be the recurrence of devastating dust storms in the Ozark Plateau. Moreover, solar disturbances can cause major disruptions in our prevailing social systems by disturbing electronic communications, including satellite transmissions.

Environmental crises in some of their present forms have long been with us. We have early accounts of general famine in the Old Testament in Joseph's interpretation of Pharaoh's dreams. There are written records of famine in China over a period of 2,000 years. Forecasts of severe famine in more modern times range from the predictions of Malthus to those made by the Paddock brothers in *Famine-1975*. The scenario for the collapse of our global civilization as a result of food and other environmental crises has recently been dramatically presented by the Meadows group in their World 3 global systems model described in *The Limits to Growth,* not incidentally by any means universally accepted as a valid simulation of our present world system.

More specific descriptions of past environmental crises have been presented in papers by R. S. Lopez, among others, and several of the contributors to this volume. Traditionally we in our industrial civilizations have come to believe as a matter of faith that all such crises belong to the past. We consider that today any environmental crisis can be overcome by introducing some appropriate technological fix. For example, the present administration of the United States appears to believe, as did its more recent predecessors, that our current environmental dilemmas can be resolved by the selection and use of appropriate technologies. They are strongly supported in this supposition by a selection of the scientific community of whom Herman Kahn is but one of the better known examples.

We can represent this belief or paradigm that technology will always find a way with a simple graphic model (see figure 1.1). This model was developed several years ago. It illustrates that as long as our society is extracting a total of resources from the environment sufficient to satisfy our current necessities, we will not be stimulated to employ new extractive technologies, however many of these have been discovered. We have accumulated an enormous bank of inventions, most of which will remain unutilized until some new crisis happens along and demands their adoption. Thus, many societies retained sledges, for example in Malta and Central Africa, long after

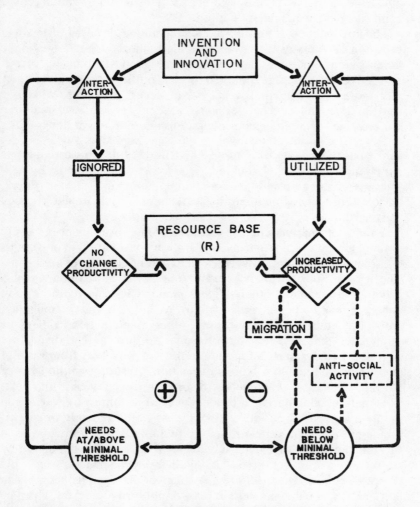

FIGURE 1.1:   When resource availability has fallen below the minimal threshold, technological innovations are utilized to increase extractive capacity. As indicated, this feedback mechanism is avoided by migration to an unexploited area or seizure of resources from other populations or population segments.   From A. S. Boughey, "World Population Growth - A General Model," *International Journal of Environmental Studies,* 7 (1974).

they must have been made aware of the use of the wheel. Australian aborigines remained hunter-gatherers despite their contact over centuries with seagoing agriculturalists.

The introduction of new extraction techniques is perhaps the most common single way we have responded when our resources have fallen below our needs and necessities. Such stepping up of our extractive capacity inevitably damages our environment further. Yet more environmental damage can occur, however, when we opt for a second alternative. This is when we decide to maintain our existing technologies but migrate to another as yet unexploited region. This second maneuver is what perhaps could best be described as the *frontier approach*. The United States in particular has experienced successive degradations of its virgin lands by fur-trappers, ranchers, sod-busters, lumbermen, miners, and others, who without changing their basic technologies marched steadily westward over a previously unexploited continent.

A third alternative when resources become insufficient is merely to help oneself to someone else's. This is a possibility that most of us consider a daily threat, hovering like a thundercloud over our heads. The effort to forestall such an event drains away more of our surplus productivity than any other single demand. The majority of us go in constant fear of being ripped off by robbery, burglary, mugging, extortion, embezzlement, or some other manipulation, violent or otherwise, that depletes our personal resources. Nationally we devote enormous sums of money to protect ourselves from wars of aggression that would rob us of our national resources although—or perhaps because—we ourselves resorted to this device in the past. This method of acquiring additional needed resources by war, while theoretically outlawed internationally, was until recently organized as a legitimate procedure, and we still retain many resources won in this manner. Thus the western hemisphere came to be populated by Europeans several centuries ago, and in this same manner California was added to the United States. Portions of the continents of Africa and many parts of Asia were at least temporarily annexed. Even as recently as the oil crisis of 1973-74 there were unauthenticated rumors that the United States might revert to this method of overcoming any oil resource deficit and send in the marines.

All three of these alternatives, technological change, migration, and annexation, represent population response to environmental crisis arising from resource shortages when we have exceeded a given area's human carrying capacity. Ecologists use the term *carrying capacity* to indicate the maximum level at which a population can extract sufficient total resources from the environment to satisfy its population necessities. Our own human populations, like any other animal populations, have specific relationships with this carrying capacity limit. These have been variously described in the past by different authors, and their social significance has most recently been explored by William Ophuls in *Ecology and the Politics of Scarcity*.

Because we have built-in time lags in our population processes, human populations are very likely to overshoot their carrying capacity. For one thing, there is a nine-month gestation period; for another, full resource needs do not develop until after adolescence, say, at age sixteen. In many nations more than half the population is below this age; so additional demands will be imposed on carrying capacity simply by these juveniles as they mature, even without any further increase in numbers. We can thus easily generate famine conditions in instances where our populations have inadvertently increased to the point where when mature they will exceed the carrying capacity in food production. This indeed is the type of disaster about which Malthus warned; it was one of Paul Ehrlich's messages in *The Population Bomb,* and it was a part of the basis for the Paddock brothers' predictions in *Famine-1975*. It was one of the reasons why Garrett Hardin developed his "Living on a Lifeboat" analogy.

Authorities are currently about equally divided between those who believe that, given adequate means of food distribution, we shall not in the next century or so overshoot our carrying capacity in terms of our food needs, and those who believe that unforeseen or unpredictable events, such as a cycle of bad weather, will shortly find us with insufficient food on a global scale. We have recently received warning from Lester Brown and his World Watch Institute that mortality in some areas is beginning to rise. This might well signal these particular populations' close approach to their food carrying capacity.

Unfortunately, food is not the only limiting factor on the carrying capacity of human populations. Fresh water is obviously another, as we are once again being most forcibly reminded in some areas of the United States. In countries like Saudi Arabia, where water is the principal limiting factor, we find almost incredible schemes under serious consideration, such as the towing of icebergs from the Antarctic to equatorial waters, where they will melt to form reservoirs of fresh water. In the Soviet Union it is proposed to reverse the flow of a major river, the Ob, using atomic blasts. Our industrial activities in their turn are clearly limited by resources of certain mineral ores, quite apart from fossil fuels, to which we will return later. In the United States we allowed a shortage of chromium temporarily to override our political convictions. The Japanese literally move mountains of iron ore from Mauritania and Swaziland to satisfy the needs of their steel industry. The United States has made not too creditable financial deals with countries like Ghana in order to obtain cheap sources of aluminum. However we regard such studies as those of the Meadows World 3 model, it is apparent even to the most skeptical that we have insufficient mineral resources to permit the complete industrialization of the approximately six billion human population that we shall have in the next millenium using our currently established technologies. To meet coming shortages we can change our technologies appropriately or we can annex those of other peoples, but only a relatively few of us will be able to migrate, for the last frontiers are fast disappearing. There are signs that instead of relying on one or more of these three strategies so far described, we might adopt instead at this point a fourth and radically different procedure. *Rather than struggle for more resources for our expanding populations, we might voluntarily reduce population growth.*

When we discuss population control, we must bring into consideration the idea of an *optimum population.* The concept of carrying capacity, defined as the asymptote where a given resource or resources is just adequate for the needs of a population that has reached a specific size, provides a simplistic model for a human population. As has already been noted, time lags commonly intervene to prevent the population from remaining at this size and level of demand. Instead, for some time mathematical demographers have used a graphic model to display a relationship that more closely approaches reality (see figure 1.2). There are three points in this model at which successively increasing population size can be theoretically determined, labeled N_1, N_2, and N_3. In figure 1.2, N_2, the *maximum sustainable population,* is the point coinciding with the maximum population size at carrying capacity. At this point, all the extracted resources, that is, all the productivity, is utilized to meet population necessities. It is possible for a population to continue growth beyond this point only if it consumes, in addition to its productivity, some of the resources of production itself. This increased population size cannot be maintained, however; it must suffer Malthusian attrition. Thus a traditional Eskimo group, faced with a population too large to carry it through the winter, could put some older persons and female infants out on the ice. Or it could consume its sled dogs. The latter course of action would momentarily enable the population to remain above the carrying capacity, but shortly all would perish because productivity could not be maintained without the dogs.

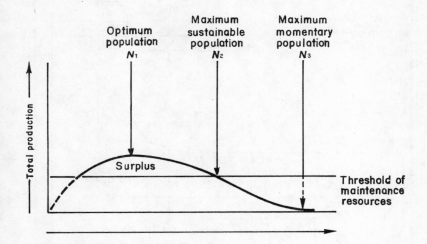

.FIGURE 1.2: HUMAN CARRYING CAPACITIES. There are three definable carrying capacity limits, identified in this diagram as N1, N2, and N3; the first two are at equilibrium points, and N3 is a momentary position. N1 is the optimum population at the peak of production before the law of diminishing returns has begun to operate; surplus productivity is at a maximum. N2 is the population when total production balances the minimum maintenance production necessary to sustain the system. The population maximum can rise beyond this to N3 but only at the expense of the production necessary to maintain the system.

There is a period before the population reaches N_2, the maximum sustainable population, when productivity is so high that there is what anthropologists describe as a *surplus*. The optimum population, N_1, is that which optimizes the surplus. It permits the population to support unproductive workers, such as artists, storytellers, scribes, priests, warriors, orators, rulers, and bureaucrats. Economists have long defined the optimum population as the point of maximum individual productivity, which is the same thing. Later, we shall consider what happens in this model if the non-productive element uses more of the productivity than the amount actually in the surplus.

Yet another concept to be taken into account in discussing population control is that of *feedback mechanisms*. About fifty years ago

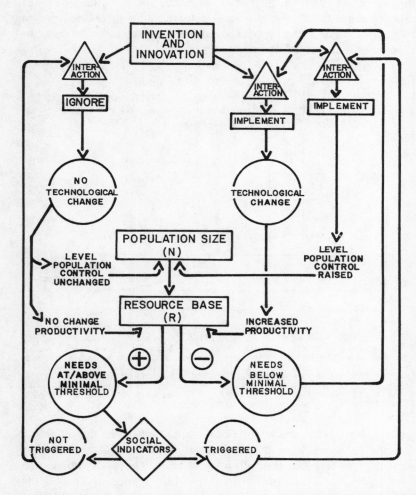

FIGURE 1.3: THE SOCIAL INDICATOR FEEDBACK MECHANISM. This mechanism holds a "K" mode population in steady-state at zero population growth and within its resource base. If social indicators are lost, the mechanism becomes inoperative, and the population switches to an "r" phase. From A. S. Boughey, "World Population Growth - A General Model," *International Journal of Environmental Studies,* 7 (1974).

an English economist, Sir Alexander Carr-Saunders, suggested that human populations had cultural mechanisms that prevented them from exceeding their carrying capacities and thereby encountering Malthusian disasters. He did not, however, specify these cultural mechanisms, nor did later workers like Wynne-Edwards who further extended his thesis. The graphic model in figure 1.3 developed several years ago suggests that human populations have a group of social indicators that enables the population to sense when it is approaching a particular carrying capacity limit.

The way social indicators could work in regulating natural increase can be illustrated by a simple theoretical example. Suppose a hypothetical tribal group has a traditional practice requiring a suitor to present his prospective father-in-law with one hundred ostrich feathers. These will be used in decorating his torso when he turns up at tribal dances. If one hundred feathers are not produced, the marriage is off. As the tribal group increases in size, the number of intending spouses increases, and the local ostrich population, which is not similarly increasing in size, becomes sadly depleted of tail feathers. Consequently, it takes much longer to amass a hundred feathers, marriages are delayed and the rate of natural increase is slowed, because illegitimate births in this tribal group are not permitted. A few more adventurous suitors trespass into other tribal areas seeking unexploited ostriches, and they get killed for their enterprise, thus permanently removing their reproductive potential. Many of the discouraged suitors decide to quit for the current season and try again next year, thus giving the ostriches time to grow new tailpieces. Such postponements of marriage will produce a smaller sized cohort of infants, thus placing a restriction on the rate of population growth, but permitting a return to a higher rate when this smaller cohort in its turn comes to seek ostrich feathers.

This theoretical example makes clear the distinction between a necessity and a need. Food is a necessity. When it is in short supply our populations soon run into Malthusian disasters. Ostrich feathers are a need. Without them the father of a bride may not cut such a fine figure at the tribal dance, but nobody dies from a shortage of them. More importantly, because of this early check on population growth, nobody dies as a result of overshooting the human carrying capacity.

The nature of the particular social indicators used in a given society will obviously vary with different populations; many have actually been described in recent years by anthropologists. The best known of these studies first appeared in 1967 in a book entitled *Pigs for the Ancestors,* by R. A. Rappaport, which described the relationship between a small human population in New Guinea, its social customs, the numbers of domestic pigs which it kept, and the environment. Simply stated, the numbers of domestic pigs were allowed to build up until incidents related to the damage they caused to cultivated plots became so aggravated as to provoke the outbreak of a local war. Local wars had limited casualties and were associated with periods of sexual abstinence so that mortality was increased and fertility decreased. When there had been sufficient casualties to satisfy honor, peace was declared. The former combatants together engaged in a great feast of many days' duration during which all the domestic pigs that could be seized were killed, cooked, and eaten. The whole cycle then began again.

In our own industrialized societies, it would appear that social indicators take a fairly direct economic form. Such factors as the cost of a university education, the maintenance of a large house, the loss of an income source by the mother, or even the abandonment of her career, may all serve as deterrents to high fertility at a time when population is pressing so hard against its resources as to make all such social needs very costly.

To pursue the question of the existence of such social indicators at various societal levels, the possibility of their serving as carrying capacity feedback signals, it is helpful to examine our societal evolution. In order to do this we can separate our global societies into some half dozen broad categories and then examine the frequency of environmental crises in each.

Anthropologists have begun to look at societal organizations in terms of productivity. The division of our total global society into several such ecological categories was first suggested for comparative purposes in A. S. Boughey, *Man and the Environment* (1971). The six or seven categories indicated in figure 1.4 represent the development of social organization during some four or five million years of evolution in our genus *Homo*. Although we commonly accept three or four different species within this genus, all are considered now extinct except for our present form, *Homo sapiens sapiens*. It is in this form alone that men have adapted to any other mode of existence than that of hunter-gatherers. About a hundred thousand years ago, when our own species was first emerging, all men were hunter-gatherers. Despite the enormous increase in population size since that time, there are now probably fewer hunter-gatherer people than existed then.

The carrying capacity of the earth for hunter-gatherers is low. Their cultures are now rapidly being invaded by alien influences. It

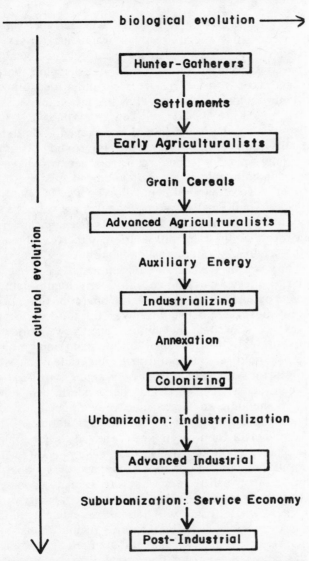

FIGURE 1.4: SOCIETAL EVOLUTION IN THE GENUS HOMO. Both biological and cultural evolution have occurred simultaneously in man over approximately 5 million years, but only during the 100,000 years of our present species *Homo sapiens sapiens* have there been quantum cultural changes. The new categories of society that appeared were the consequence of cultural changes that removed previous impediments to the optimization of population density. These technologies once evolved could readily be copied, given the appropriate resources, so that the process of societal evolution became transformed into one of societal succession. Some attempts to shorten this successional process invariably failed. For example, colonizing societies established directly from advanced agricultural societies invariably collapsed eventually.

is very difficult to assess in this century whether they or our hunter-gatherer ancestors encountered environmental crises that were controlled by cultural feedbacks until technological improvements raised carrying capacity limits. We imagine that the evolution of hand axes from pebble tools permitted dense human populations. Anthropologists consider that the introduction of the spear thrower and of fire would do likewise. We have as yet, however, little evidence that our populations reached a Malthusian carrying capacity before adopting these improved extraction methods. Generally speaking, hunter-gatherers seem to have led somewhat brief, but enjoyable, lives, maintaining adequate resource levels by some practice of cultural population control, probably by female infanticide. Traditionally Eskimo populations were kept in check by this control method, but such a practice appears more likely to have been a direct response to a perceived threat of starvation than a feedback from a social indicator.

It is likely that when they faced an environmental crisis because they threatened to exceed carrying capacity early hunter-gatherer bands would have opportunity to exercise the migration alternative. Tribal bands also must have constantly taken the third option and ravaged the resources of their neighbors. The New World and Australia were virgin territories open to the land migration of hunter-gatherers without sea transport other than crude rafts. Work such as P. S. Martin's book on *Pleistocene extinctions* has suggested that when our species invaded the western hemisphere and Australia, it encountered large game prey fauna unused to hunting by human predators. Uncontrolled exploitation of this abundant and convenient food resource is believed to have finally resulted in the phenomenon known as *Pleistocene overkill,* which about twelve thousand years ago so greatly depleted the numbers of many large animals in North America and drove many species to extinction. It is difficult to imagine that the carrying capacity of the Paleo-Indian hunter-gatherer bands was not correspondingly reduced by the early environmental crisis that this would constitute. Mortality in inclement seasons, especially infant mortality and death among juveniles, must have risen considerably at such a time; perhaps, too, some cultural feedbacks evolved that tended to reduce the birth rate. Shortages of food may have extended the nursing period of infants to three years or more, thereby spacing out births to four or five-year intervals, as has been observed among modern bushmen. This paleolithic environmental crisis probably persisted until agricultural techniques were introduced, thereby raising the food carrying capacity and permitting the support of larger human population densities.

The agricultural revolution that occurred in several regions of Eurasia about fifteen thousand years ago, and a little later in the western hemisphere, permitted the succession of human populations to the second societal category, *early agriculturalists*, or *gardeners*, as they are known to anthropologists. It is believed that the agricultural revolution did not *permit* settlement so much as that settlements developed and then the agricultural revolution became associated with them. Hunter-gatherer settlements are known; they may have arisen because local carrying capacities were exceptionally high owing to the existence of a seasonal diversity of nearby extractable ecosystems, permitting the establishment of permanent settlements. Previous to this, hunter-gatherer bands had been forced to move constantly in the course of their nomadic peregrinations because carrying capacity became temporarily reduced in each locality after occupations lasting no more than days or weeks.

Early agriculturalists, especially those in forested areas, depended more particularly on cultivated fruits and root crops. The capacity of the land to maintain constant cropping with such plants would deteriorate after a number of years. It would be necessary to move on to an unexploited or regenerated area in a process that is known as *swidden agriculture* or *shifting cultivation*. The work of Rappaport on population control in a group of New Guinea early agriculturalists has already been mentioned. There are a number of quite similar accounts, all describing the use by early agriculturalists of social indicators to maintain an optimum population and thereby avoid periodic environmental crises. As in the case of the hunter-gatherer category, these mechanisms related especially to death control.

It was not until the agricultural development of cultivated cereal grains that the energetics of agricultural production were sufficiently high for settlements to become potentially permanent. Cereal grains, unlike most of the fruit and root crops developed by early agriculturalists, would not grow in forest shade. The land had to be cleared of all other plants, but because of this very circumstance cereal grains captured more sunlight per given land area and thus provided a greater carrying capacity on the same acreage. Once cleared, there was less weed re-invasion of cultivated land than in swidden agriculture. Moreover, the recycling of wastes of one form or another could be used to help maintain yields, thus avoiding the inevitable decreasing fertility of shifting cultivation plots. As urbanization proceeded with this assistance from agricultural innovations, it seems that many traditional methods of population control were forgotten or abandoned by the new urban residents.

Cultivators of cereal grains can be called *advanced agriculturalists*. Nearly three billion people in the world still exist in this societal category. Their Third World countries currently have high rates of natural increase because immense reductions in the death rate beginning in the mid-twentieth century have not yet been associated with parallel reductions in the birth rate. Perhaps cultural methods of population control cannot cope with such an extreme population surge, even where they still linger. Thus the Third World countries are pushing continually against their carrying capacity in terms of renewable resources, especially food, and are particularly susceptible to the ravages of famines resulting from cycles of adverse weather. Because of the frequent at least temporary ineffectiveness of social indicators, their population is regulated by Malthusian death controls. Environmental crises for this category of society consist essentially of those precipitated by weather perturbation, with the exception described below.

European populations of the high Middle Ages (1300-1500) were still in the advanced agricultural stage. Historians such as A. R. Lewis record that the earlier expansionist phase of these agricultural populations did not extend into the high Middle Ages because of the closing of the medieval frontier. This limitation of further natural resource acquisition precipitated the environmental crisis of the late Middle Ages. According to medievalists, the confrontation with the medieval carrying capacity of this region resulted in Malthusian disasters. As Bowlus has pointed out with reference to Switzerland, the medieval European environmental crisis was finally overcome only by a combination of migration, technological change, and inadvertent population control through the ravages of the Black Death.

Later in this volume, Bilsky presents an entirely novel explanation of the susceptibility of some advanced agriculturalists to periodic environmental crises. It was noted earlier from figure 1.2 that in economic population theory a population size has three different values when expressed in relation to its extractive capacity or, in anthropological terms, the relative size of the surplus it produces. As shown in figure 1.2, the optimum population size may be defined as the point at which there is a maximum surplus. The law of diminishing returns reduces this amount of surplus as population density increases further and beyond this point, until there is no surplus at all. This is the point of maximum population size.

The model in figure 1.5 developed in A. Sauvy's *General Theory of Population,* a variation of the model shown in figure 1.2, indicates that avaricious, nonproductive overlords can extract more productivity than is actually produced in the form of surplus by a population of a given size. Such action soon pushes the population

Marginal Output and Standard of Living

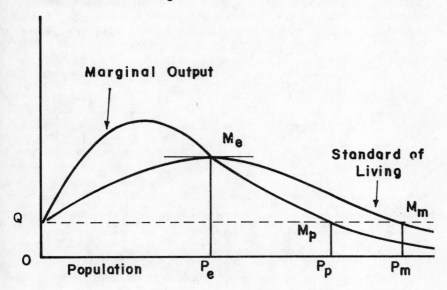

FIGURE 1.5: EXPLOITATION OF THE SURPLUS. In this diagram, which should be compared with that in figure 1.2, Sauvy calls surplus "marginal output," and charts not its gross production, but the *net* production remaining after a nonproductive power structure has removed a portion. The optimum population, Pe is that which optimizes population density and the nonproductive power structure, maximizing the standard of living. This falls as the power structure reduces net productivity to nil, at Pp, and drops below subsistence level at point Pm, where net productivity is less than maintenance value.

below its maximum sustainable point and precipitates Malthusian disasters. Thus, even without deterioration of the weather cycle an environmental crisis can occur in which, to paraphrase a translation Bilsky quotes of a fourth-century B.C. Chinese text, the *Mo-tzu,* the hungry cannot be fed, the cold cannot be clothed, and the tired cannot get rest.

As Bilsky notes, Sauvy remarks that under these overtaxed conditions, farmers try to spread the load by increasing their numbers. It is apparent, however, from the model in figure 1.5 that this maneuver will soon lead to overpopulation and will further shorten the time before the population reaches its maximum sustainable level. Bilsky relates his ideas to advanced agricultural societies, but they are applicable to any societal category in which a despotic ruling or priestly class, or an overgrown bureaucracy, extracts resources from its supportive economy that are larger than the actual surplus.

Advanced agriculturalists persist with a primitive economic system in which the sole energy supply consists of the solar radiation captured in crop plants. Until we adopted systems utilizing other sources of energy, we were permanently locked into this primitive

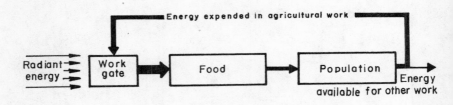

FIGURE 1.6: THE BIOENERGETIC BLOCK OF AGRARIAN ECONOMIES. An agrarian society utilizes only the radiant energy which falls as sunlight on its territory and is in part acquired in the photosynthetic process of its crop plants. As this formalized diagram shows, this bioenergetic regime is a vicious circle in which a limited number of people can be supported by the radiant energy acquired in this way; they must devote virtually the whole of the energy they obtain to raising more crops to acquire more energy for more people.

relationship, as is shown by the energetic diagram in figure 1.6. For the Third World of advanced agriculturalists, that is for a majority portion of our current human population, the present environmental crisis has resolved itself into an energy crisis. These societies need the auxiliary sources of energy that will enable them to produce the fertilizers, irrigation systems, herbicides, pesticides, and mechanical implements to raise their food carrying capacity sufficiently high so as to remove the ever present threat of famine resulting from inclement weather.

To break out of this advanced agricultural energy block our more evolved societies introduced energy from certain auxiliary sources some two or three centuries ago. At first these took the form of wind and water power. Later we utilized wood and coal, and now oil and nuclear energy. The effect of the insertion of auxiliary energy into our energetic systems is shown in figure 1.7. The human energy of the population is no longer monopolized by food raising and now can be diverted to industrial activities. Such activities are characteristic of the fourth societal category, *industrializing societies*. These arose first in Western Europe, and history best records this process in Great Britain.

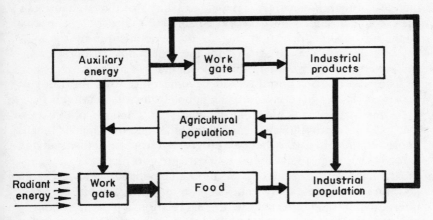

FIGURE 1.7: THE BIOENERGETIC CYCLE OF AN INDUSTRIAL SOCIETY. Once auxiliary energy supplies are inserted into the bioenergetic cycle of a society, the main activity of the population can be directed into the utilization of this energy in industrial production. Some of this industrial production and a comparatively small proportion of the population can utilize a portion of the auxiliary energy to produce food both for themselves and for the ever increasing industrial population.

Traditional population controls were not reinstated in this first group of industrializing societies. Thus, in their turn, these populations grew until they eventually encountered an environmental crisis, due in this case to insufficient resources of one form or another. One resource shortage that quickly became evident was lumber, and others developed in wool, cotton, leather, and edible oils. Food also began to become a problem as industrializing societies underwent urbanization and workers were removed from agricultural industry at a greater rate than their labor could be replaced by mechanization. In any case, some industrializing societies occupied too small a national territory to have sufficient agricultural acreage to support their burgeoning urban populations. Thus the industrializing European nations launched into many colonial adventures, annexing portions of Canada for its lumber and furs, Australia for its wool and mutton, Africa and India for lumber, cotton, peanuts, palm oil, sugar, and food of other kinds.

These industrializing societies thereby entered universally into the new societal category of *colonizing societies*. They raised the carrying capacity of their metropolitan and urbanized homelands by importing external resources required for their expanding industries. They themselves reaped the main benefit from the consequent increase in their homelands' carrying capacity, for the population of the colonized regions necessarily remained at the carrying capacity of the advanced agricultural category. The acquisition by the metropolitan populations of at least for the time ample resources continued to discourage the possible development of population control measures. Because mortality had become quite low, the rates of natural increase in these colonizing populations was very high.

In this way, some thirty-one industrializing nations of Western Europe, together with Russia as a late comer and then finally Japan, approximately fifty years behind, progressed from the industrializing category, through the colonializing category, to reach the category of *advanced industrial society*. As it became politically unacceptable and, finally, pragmatically impossible to maintain colonial empires, international trade replaced the original relationship of metropolitan country to colonial dependency. However, even in this new relationship, the original industrial nation in the advanced industrial category retained the same energetic relationships with its former colonial dependency, still locked into the advanced agricultural category. The advanced industrial nations continued to obtain food and raw mineral resources in exchange for the industrial goods which they manufactured exclusively. However, the social revolution we call the *demographic transition* had now occurred. The cost of children as compared with other amenities of the good life was weighed and found unattractive. Consequently, voluntary birth control had drastically reduced fertility and thus natural increase in all the advanced industrial nations.

Our latest and unless we move energetically to overcome it, last environmental crisis has arisen because the burgeoning industries of the world's thirty-two industrialized nations in the advanced industrial category have begun to compete with one another for mineral and fuel resources and also are now beginning to have to compete for these same items with the Third World nations. Many of these are just beginning to emerge from the advanced agricultural category into the industrializing category, and their populations have consequently been exploding and urbanizing at an unprecedented rate.

A survey of societal succession in the terms used above enables us to look analytically at our present environmental crisis and to determine in what ways, if any, it differs from the previous crises that historians have so far been able to describe for us. Our present environmental dilemma is clearly not unique in terms of its food element. In fact, many of our previous environmental crises have arisen primarily because of technical limits on food production.

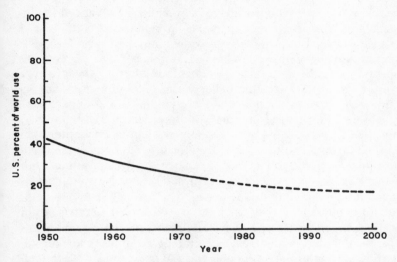

FIGURE 1.8: ACTUAL AND PROJECTED U.S. CONSUMPTION OF NONRE-NEWABLE RESOURCES ON A PROPORTIONAL WORLD BASIS. As shown in this illustration, the U.S. consumption of mineral resources, although still rising exponentially, is now a diminishing proportion of the total world use, because this also is rising exponentially. U.S. requirements are proportionally much less than the potential world demands. U.S. supplies of such resources as mica, tantalum, and tin are already exhausted; and more than 90 percent of others, such as aluminum, antimony, cobalt, and manganese, have to be imported, as do more than half of certain others, such as asbestos, cadmium, nickel, and zinc. The United States also now imports more than a third of its requirements of iron ore, lead, and mercury. Commercial and political leverage for negotiating further imports of these essential mineral resources into the United States and other industrialized countries is diminishing continuously.

It is unique in its pressure upon energy supplies. Until our time, Western Europe was able to meet all its energy needs from its coal reserves. North America, even without exhausting its coal reserves, until the mid-1950s was able to extract oil and natural gas supplies more than sufficient for its own requirements. This latest crisis is therefore unique in the first place in that our now advanced industrial and industrializing nations are encountering presently insoluble energy shortages for the first time. Discoveries of further fossil fuel energy supplies in Alaska, the Gulf of Suez, or the North Sea can do little to alleviate this situation on an ultimate basis. Moreover, modern industrializing societies, which for the most part lack their own energy supplies, have no money even to alleviate the situation on a proximate basis.

A second unique feature of this latest environment crisis arises in relation to shortages of other, non-fuel mineral resources. Previously, the thirty or so industrialized nations in the advanced industrial category had such low demands in relation to total world reserves of minerals that they have not encountered serious supply shortages. Now, as indicated in figure 1.8, which shows the ongoing proportions of U.S. mineral requirements relative to those of the rest of the world, the situation is very different and many minerals containing critical elements, such as chromium, iron, copper, mercury, aluminum, manganese, and tin, are increasingly in short supply. It is true that most of these elements can be encountered in diminished quantities in sea water or in the crustal rocks of the earth and also that elements still abundant can be substituted for them, but the technologies necessary for such extraction or substitution are as yet generally unknown or undeveloped.

The third unique feature of the present environmental crisis lies in a negative rather than a positive feature: the enormous amount of new forms of pollution now being generated. In our first two societal categories, of hunter-gatherers and early agriculturalists, such degradation of renewable resources of the local environment as occurred was generally soon remedied by regeneration once we abandoned the area. Even in our advanced agricultural societies, while such degradation was permanent, extensive pollution was avoided. Although smoke from domestic fires would cause localized air pollution with particulate matter, and streams for some distance might suffer cultural eutrophication, the organic wastes and combustion products of these societies in general were recycled on the land. No new chemical substances were introduced to the environment.

With industrialization all this has changed. Organic wastes are discharged into our ecosystems at rates far beyond the ability of natural buffering and cleansing systems to clear. Moreover, entirely new chemical substances, such as polyethylene, fluorocarbons, organophosphates, polynated biphenols, and a host of other substances generated by our burgeoning chemical industries, are released. Together with these are quantities of familiar elements, such as sulfur, mercury, and vanadium, which until recently were comparatively rare as free elements in natural ecosystems. The splitting of the atom has resulted not only in increases in the amounts of tritium, deuterium, and many naturally occurring radioactive isotopes but also in the synthesis of previously totally unrepresented ones, such as the extremely toxic plutonium.

The best solution to this unique pollution aspect of the environmental crisis is perhaps the simplest. Industrial technology has created this monster; industrial technology can remove it. However, such action seems to be a matter of economic trade-offs. What we will accept in the form of chemical and physical environmental pollution varies with the relative shortages of material goods and other resources whose production leads to the pollution. Happily, numerous examples can be found where ultimate environmentalist views have triumphed over material proximate ones. The British have cleaned up the air over London and the tidal waters of the River Thames; Oregonians likewise have restored the Williamette River, and Pittsburghians can once more see clearly through the air of their city.

A fourth element of our present environmental crisis is not perhaps unique in its occurrence, but it is certainly unprecedented in its scale: the rate at which we are degrading the renewable and nonrenewable resources of our planet. At the present rate, urban sprawl soon will cover the whole landscape. The rich ecological diversity of this planet, with its almost infinite communities of plants and animals, will have been reduced to a number of weed species together with a few overbred cultivated plants and domestic animals. Countries like the United States, which by historical chance still have some considerable stretches of relatively undisturbed land, have made distinct progress in regulating its continuing preservation. However, when some critical shortage develops, of natural gas, oil, water, or some other resource, the environmentalists are usually overridden in favor of the developers. It is ironic that since the days when William the Conqueror established a royal hunting preserve in England's New Forest, the most consistent conservation of remaining natural areas has been practiced by monarchs, dictators, the military, and racial supremacist governments. In this latest environmental crisis, democratic governments too often are forced to set the conspicuous resource needs of the people above the less directly obvious benefits from the preservation of undisturbed natural areas.

The population problem is not unique to our present environmental dilemma—we have faced it many times before. Having survived this far, we have developed cultural mechanisms, as yet little understood, that caused us when necessary to diminish the rate of natural increase. Some groups, like most nations of Western Europe, are currently approaching the stationary population level. A few, such as the two Germanies, have a negative rate of natural increase. All national populations presently show a decline in their rate of natural increase.

It appears that our present environmental crisis cannot be resolved ultimately until we have developed an abundant, pollution-free source of cheap energy. Whether this will come from the use of solar radiation, the atomic fusion of lighter chemical elements, such as deuterium, or the exploitation of geothermal power is not yet clear. Meanwhile, extension of the industrial nations' proximate use of conventional energy sources, such as coal, oil, natural gas, and hydro-electric constructions, linked with appropriate energy conserving economies is the only way in which such nations can survive without major economic change. Simultaneously, such measures will permit us to embark upon the long process of industrialization in the underdeveloped Third World. Greater amounts of energy in this proximate consideration will have to be diverted to pollution control and the recycling and re-use of critical mineral resources; in the end, vast quantities of energy will be required for these two purposes if we are not to degrade our planet utterly. We will, in fact, have to pass from the growth ethic, which in two hundred years carried America forward to become the dominant industrial power, to an *environmental ethic*. In a paper which appears later in this volume, Moneyhon has demonstrated that this realization was present among progressive thinkers even before World War I. However, as Boughey has recently pointed out in "A Letter on Ecological Ethic—California Experience," the U.S. population as a whole does not yet appear ready to abandon the growth ethic.

There remains only the sociological element of our current crisis, and this problem is unique to advanced industrialized societies. In no other societal categories do we currently encounter such appalling levels of social dysfunction. It is possible that cities in fully industrialized societies have now served their purpose and may eventually become as extinct as temporary hunter-gatherer groups. In the United States, cities are increasingly being rejected. New York's economic difficulties persist, and already some thirty other major cities are in financial trouble; their rates of crime, unemployment, malnutrition, and other social problems unbelievable. Of the twenty-six largest cities in the United States, twenty are currently showing a net population loss, despite a still positive rate of natural increase in the country at large.

In the United States, more of us live in suburbs than in inner cities; Australia and certain other countries likewise. It seems that cities reached their zenith in the colonizing societal category. Advanced industrial societies are better characterized by suburbs rather than cities as the favored type of settlement pattern for several reasons. When we move, as we are now doing, into a seventh category of societal organization, the *post-industrial society,* it will be characterized, as Meadows and others have pointed out, by the preponderance of service industries as compared with production enterprises. Perhaps it will also be characterized by new dwelling arrangements. In these, better resource distribution will ensure that such crimes as robbery and embezzlement, which arise largely from resource scarcity, will diminish or disappear. More egalitarian resource distribution will not, however, dispel all the social dysfunctions that typify our present environmental crisis. It would appear that further social changes must occur.

What these social changes may be we can only at present speculate. During the last hundred years or so in the industrialized nations we have managed to deflect our sexual drive entirely away from its main purpose. Its universal primary function now is, as in a lion pride, not so much to initiate reproduction of the species as to maintain social contentment within the system. It may be that the urgent drive of parenthood may likewise, at least in part and for some, be similarly deflected from biological to cultural immortality. In industrial societies, from one-third to one-quarter of us now elect to remain clinically sterile. As many sociobiological authors have described, we appear to have an innate drive to package our own genes and pass them on as undiluted as possible to future generations. This objective of parenthood was presumably developed by natural selection to ensure that we did not just stop at copulation once our sexual drive was satisfied. With the need now to recognize the finiteness of global resources, it has become urgent to contain our reproduction to replacement values. For many individuals this will mean a childless existence. At best, it will involve us as parents for a mere quarter of our lives or less. It is possible that we will be satisfied with contributing to the preservation of our own genes to the extent that they are represented in our kinfolk. If so, to achieve a more personal immortality we must turn to some characteristic or innovative cultural development. Our heavy involvement with the continuing survival of *artifacts, sociofacts,* or *mentifacts* may replace our innate drive for gene bank propagation.

If this is to be the case, we might with the end of resource shortages after the present crisis is over also see the end of the various social dysfunctions that have seriously aggravated the latest environmental crisis. With the removal of resource scarcities, the avoidance of pollution, and the re-direction of primary innate reproductive drives, human societies might for the first time in their history look forward to a future unclouded by any threat of imminent environmental disaster.

CHAPTER TWO

Prehistoric Ecological Crises

by Michael P. Hoffman

Archeologists or prehistorians have some advantages when it comes to perspectives on ecological crises. We are able to take broad views because our interests range over a tremendous span of time (99 percent of human existence) and space (any place inhabited by humans). There are also disadvantages, which are usually caused by the limited preservation of archeological data and the difficulty of confirmation of interpretations of the past. In this paper, I want to use our knowledge of prehistory and anthropology to discuss ecological crises in our past and what kinds of currently relevant generalities may emerge from them.

First we have to know what an ecological crisis is. We would all probably define it somewhat differently. Since anthropologists have to deal with people anytime, anywhere, I will take a broad view of an ecological crisis. Human societies are parts of large ecosystems. They are merely subsystems in a general natural system consisting of many parts—energy from the sun, plants, animals, water, elements of the terrain, and many others—which interact complexly. Some parts of the system are always changing, and this change affects other parts. Looking at it ethnocentrically, rapid change affecting one part of this system and in turn strongly affecting a human adaptation, or vice versa, constitutes an ecological crisis. The primary cause of the crisis can be "natural" or "human" to make an arbitrary division. Thus Upper Paleolithic reindeer hunters in Holland must have thought it a crisis when their best hunting lands were inundated at the end of the Pleistocene by the rising sea levels caused by glacial retreat (a "natural" cause), and the Maya in

the Peten must have thought it a crisis when, because of overcultivation, hard-to-cultivate grassland took root where there had been
tropical forest before (a "human" cause and a debatable interpretation).

Prehistoric ecological crises can be disastrous to human populations, creating hunger, disease and/or out-migration, or they can be
"creative" in the sense that they help to cause new productive
human adaptations in the same basic environment but with new
technology, food sources, or other sources of energy. A good
example of a disastrous prehistoric situation was the demise of the
Harappan civilization in the Indus Valley. One popular explanation
for the end of the advanced urban culture there involves deforestation of the valley to obtain fuel to fire bricks and consequent erosion
and flooding. Another involves a natural dam on the Indus, created
by tectonic movement, a barrier which eventually flooded
Mohenjo-Daro.

Latest theories on the origin of the agricultural revolution in the
Near East can be argued on a "creative" ecological crisis basis.
Between ten and twenty thousand years ago in favored parts of the
Near East a combination of new food sources (wild grasses such as
wheat, wild herd animals, riverine and lacustrine resources) and
improved technology resulted in a semi-sedentary "good life" for
Natufian peoples of the upland Levant. However, with increased
sedentism it became easier for women to raise several children at the
same time, and population increased. The optimum resource zone of
the Levant was limited in extent, and an ecological crisis occurred
for the expanding Natufian population. Small groups of Natufians
were forced into marginal resource zones where the "good life"
could not be maintained with the same technology because of less
luxurious natural food resources. They began to protect, maintain,
concentrate on, and eventually cultivate wheat in an effort to
produce adequate food for their expanding population. Thus Near
Eastern agriculture was born, and it in turn laid the basis for more
"creative" crises leading up to the present.

When humans have been responsible for ecological crises, both
prehistorically and today, overpopulation has been a key culprit.
The human animal, like any other, has tremendous potential fertility
and, given unrestrained reproduction, can outstrip any ecological
system in a short time. However, all human societies, yesterday and
today, have devised means of restricting reproduction so actual
population increases are far less than the potential. Disease has also
played a part, of course.

In prehistoric and contemporary tribal populations, particularly those that live by hunting and gathering, high infant mortality, child-spacing mechanisms, such as sexual continence, abortion, and selective (usually female) infanticide, keep population increases low. In hunting and gathering groups population is (was) often about 30 percent of environmental carrying capacity (which is a loaded relative term) because of the reasons above and because mobility restricted the number of infants or young children a woman could handle. Left to themselves, hunting and gathering people usually don't create clear-cut ecological crises in spite of the fact that they are not the primitive ecologists some romantics in our society think they are (examples are multitudes of Plains hunters who slaughtered bison in droves and utilized only minor quantities of their kills). However, the evidence is that there were small but steady population increases which in millennia resulted in the necessity in certain areas to develop new food resources.

In tribal agricultural societies, incessant warfare emerges as a means of population control, usually not directly in numbers of people killed, but in installing a male chauvinism complex which denigrates the role of women and justifies widespread female infanticide. Significant proportions of adult males are killed, however.

Any factors that change native population control mechanisms create potential ecological crises due to overpopulation. Agriculture or some other new food source that stimulates sedentism allows women to care for several infants or young children at once. In peasant societies, more children and larger families allow more labor investment in intensive cultivation and thus create the justification for larger families. Conversion to the Christian religion with its abhorrence of infanticide and abortion releases native population controls and, coupled with Western medicine, reduces infant and childhood deaths, and an overpopulation ecological crisis results. This is happening in Africa and South America now and has happened many times before with the spread of Western European technology, political control, and belief systems. Thus, in Philippine Mindanao, these factors are responsible for population increase, the shortening of the fallow periods in slash and burn agriculture and the consequent increase in the area of infertile grassland areas.

Let us now turn to a detailed consideration of four prehistoric ecological crises, the first of them in early North American prehistory. According to Paul S. Martin in "The Discovery of America," a controversial *Science* magazine article which appeared in 1973, the early migrants to the New World were responsible for wiping out the megafauna (now extinct large mammals) of the North American continent in a period of about six hundred years, a situation which could be considered an ecological crisis. According to his interpretation, early big game hunters, crossing from Siberia into the New World, came upon large animal populations which were easy to kill since they had not experienced human predation before. This ready availability of food stimulated a population explosion. He visualized the rapid spread of relatively numerous hunters (one person per square mile) in kinds of extinction fronts, overkilling the large animals until an area was cleaned out and then moving on to a new frontier where the process was repeated. There was a dense human population on the front and a sparse one behind the front. Martin devised a predation model which indicates that the "front" populations could easily have removed enough large animal biomass for quick extinction to occur. It is assumed in his study that the New World migrants were primarily big game hunters who cared little for edible plants or small animals. By quick movements following the diminishing megafauna the tip of South America was reached in just two thousand years. After the megafauna was gone profound human adaptations to a more diversified gathering, hunting, and fishing life had to occur, and population density is thought to have been less than on the densely populated extinction fronts.

This study is difficult to believe, and indeed most archeologists do not think that human predation was the root cause of late Pleistocene animal extinction in the New World. Habitat reduction is thought to have been an important factor. Also, it goes against the grain of our folk belief that tribal peoples are somehow more noble, more conservation-oriented than present day Americans or Europeans. A letter of response to Martin's article, however, gives an example of rapid overkill partly by Indians in relatively recent times. There were 48 million wild cattle in the South American pampas in 1700, but fifty years later they were almost all gone. Indians and other South Americans hunted them extensively and intensively for hides. In addition, "each Indian killed two pregnant cows a day in order to eat the unborn calves, which were considered a delicacy."[1] It is difficult to find a noble conservation ethic in that practice. I don't want to imply here that native or tribal peoples were "bad guys" or worse than modern Americans in this regard. I do wish to point out that ecological excess which results in crises as I have defined them is not only a "White folks" phenomenon. There is usually a matter of scale, however, since most tribal peoples do not have the numbers or technology to make the great scale changes which pervade several areas of the U.S. environment today.

A second example concerns the protohistoric Vikings in Greenland who were victims of an ultimate ecological crisis, one which caused their extinction. In a very cold area such as Greenland, which is marginal for human habitation in the best of times, small temperature or moisture fluctuations can be disastrous, particularly if new technological adaptations (such as snowmobiles) are not available.

The Viking expansion westward from Scandinavia first occurred in a relatively warm climatic interval which peaked in 800-1000. Eric the Red discovered Greenland for Europeans in 982. At that time the southern coastal areas had large areas of lush green pastures, with a longer growing season than present and apparently no permanently frozen ground. Norse farms were established in two major settlement areas, one near the southern tip of Greenland (the Eastern Settlement) and the other some distance up the west coast (the Western Settlement). The farmers lived by stock raising—pasturing the sheep, cattle, horses, and pigs on the rich pastures— supplemented by fishing and hunting. The products of the animals—milk, butter, and wool—were human staples. The Norse became Christianized and were able to model themselves after village life in their native Scandinavia. Population was at least 3,000. (Incidentally, the Vikings kept their population in check by infanticide.) Wood and iron were imported from Norway and the sea trade was essential.

After 1200, the climate deteriorated from the perspective of the Viking adaptation. The deterioration is viewed as a "normal" or "natural" phenomenon related ultimately to solar, astronomical, or oceanic cyclical events. The ice pack increased in size, permafrost was present and the growing season became shorter. Sea ice making communication with Norway difficult and, at times, impossible for hundreds of years, the iron and wood trade was cut off. The farmers' traditional food supplies must have been insufficient, for by 1400 cemeteries indicate that the average height was only 5'1" as opposed to the average male height 200 years before of 5'7". The Greenland Vikings may have tried to shift their economic base to predominately fishing and hunting, but in doing so they came into ecological competition with the newly arrived Eskimo populations and clashes resulted. By 1340 the Norse Western Settlement had disappeared. By 1500 the Eastern Settlement was gone and the Vikings were extinct in the whole of Greenland. When Greenland was rediscovered by Europeans in the late 1500s, the Norse were remembered only in Eskimo myths.

No one knows exactly what happened to the last Vikings in Greenland. They could have sailed away to the west; they could have been exterminated by Eskimos or absorbed genetically by the Eskimos; they could have all starved. However, we do know that the colder climate beginning in the 1200s affected them catastrophically.

For our third example, we turn to the American Southwest. Most people have heard of the abandonment of large areas of the Pueblo (or Anasazi) culture in the 1100-1300 period. Large areas of northeastern Arizona, southwestern Colorado, and northwestern New Mexico inhabited by intensive agriculturalists living in apartment-style adobe or stone pueblo villages (like Pueblo Bonito and the Mesa Verde area) were abandoned, and only a few scattered areas of pueblo people survived. Hypotheses to explain this abandonment are many, unproved, and seemingly conflicting—drought, disease, warfare, seasonal change.

Martin and Plog's *The Archaeology of Arizona,* however, offers an elegant new explanation which incorporates some of the earlier hypotheses in a coherent way but is still partly untested. Anasazi populations increased rapidly on all sections of the Colorado Plateau in the Pueblo area in the later part of the first millenium A.D. Estimates of increases range between 400 and 4000 percent between 850 and 1050. Presumably increased agricultural productivity and increased sedentism functioned to loosen previous cultural population controls. Pueblos, large and small, were sprinkled across the landscape, their inhabitants dependent on the farming of corn, beans and squash. As the population increased, new communities were forced to "bud off" from established pueblos in favorable areas to inhabit marginal land with less rainfall, less favorable floodwater farming land, less fertility, or a different growing season. The marginal pueblos still maintained trade or exchange relationships with the nuclear pueblos.

There were environmental stresses in the Southwest between 1100 and 1300 which created what must have been an ecological crisis from the Pueblo peoples' points of view. Pollen analysis indicates a shift in rainfall pattern to large amounts in late summer downpours but lesser amounts in the early summer when crops were growing and a winter drought. Erosion of deep arroyos caused by the downpours and perhaps reinforced by overcultivation resulted in a

PART TWO

THE ECOLOGY OF THE ANCIENT WORLD

Introduction

by Edward M. Anson

The two essays in this section deal with the ancient civilizations of two societies, divergent in both geography and culture but sharing common ecological problems. Both studies are indicative of a new ecological perspective in ancient history and, consequently, are concerned with the attitudes and policies exhibited by these ancient peoples in their interactions with their environment. Professor Hughes in the first essay has examined the surviving works of Greek and Roman antiquity in search of attitudes similar to those of the current "ecology" movement, and he has found many ancients "who recognized the importance of the natural environment, saw the dangers involved in the misuse of nature, and exerted themselves to preserve, protect, conserve, and enhance the natural world." And yet, as the author points out, despite numerous religious sanctions, philosophic and scientific observations, and frequent protestations, the environmental deterioration of the Mediterranean basin was not halted; it was not even slowed.

The problem, as shown in Professor Hughes's chapter, is that those elements of ancient Greco-Roman civilization which should have protected the environment of the Mediterranean world from harm were negated by other elements. For example, while there did derive from primitive Greek and Roman religion a general reluctance to tamper with nature for fear of offending the gods, Greco-Roman practicality united with universal human greed to render this apparent safeguard inoperative. Certain places, *temenē*, came to be regarded as reserved for deities, with the rest of the countryside, in consequence, being considered less sacred and more subject to human whim. Moreover, regardless of divergent philosophic and scientific opinions, it was Aristotle's concept of nature and man's relationship to nature which most closely reflected classical thought. Since for Aristotle all nature is for "the sake of man," his views, especially as interpreted by the Romans, became an invitation for environmental conquest. Following the Aristotelean idea of nature, environmental ills were avoided by bringing new land under cultivation, cutting new forests, and farming more marginal lands, rather than corrected through conservation. Consequently, the environmental deterioration of the Greco-Roman world continued unabated.

The second essay, by Professor Bilsky, is a study of an effective societal response to environmental crisis. The author argues that the Chinese in their pre-imperial history were faced with ecological problems which interacted with social, political, and economic forces to produce the Ch'in empire. Moreover, Professor Bilsky suggests that the emergence of Ch'in was not only a response to an ecological crisis but, indeed, its solution. While the new imperial government did not create much that was new, through the implementation of extensive social controls the Chinese were able to avoid much of the environmental damage meted out to the Mediterranean basin in antiquity. Professor Bilsky's study of ancient China suggests that through enforced conservation ecological crises may be avoided, but only with the loss of considerable personal freedom.

In fact, these two chapters present a paradox for modern Western civilization. Can ecological disaster be avoided, given the Western tradition of a homocentric universe, as stated so clearly by Aristotle, and the emphasis on individual initiative, or will our reaction to the symptoms of mounting environmental decay be those of the Greeks and Romans? In short, the paradox facing Western man may be that to save his society and culture from environmental chaos he himself must destroy that very society and culture.

CHAPTER THREE

Early Greek and Roman Environmentalists

by J. Donald Hughes

When Alexander the Great was in India, Plutarch tells us, he tried to pose difficult questions to some Indian philosophers. Of one he asked, "Which animal is the most cunning?" The gymnosophist was quick with his reply: "That one which men have not yet discovered."[1]

No modern defender of endangered species could have made the point more succinctly. The classical writer was aware of an apparent enmity between men and the other animals in which mankind is dominator or destroyer and the others slaves or victims. This prevailing attitude toward animals of those who share the tradition of Greece and Rome is only one aspect of the "great divorce" between mankind and nonhuman nature that looms so large in the history of Western thought. In an earlier article, "Ecology in Ancient Greece" in *Inquiry* (1975), I have tried to trace in ancient history some roots of the dominant Western attitude toward nature. In this essay, I will attempt to investigate ideas and practices which, if not dominant, were potentially more constructive.

Four sets of attitudes are to be considered here. First, one based on certain conceptions of the gods and their relationship to man will be examined. A Greek or Roman deity embodied a complex of traditional attitudes and practices, some of them exceedingly ancient and ingrained in the lives of the people of classical times. The gods invested aspects of nature with sanctity and gave their protection to segments of the natural world.

Everyone knows that the gods were spirits of nature. The god of the sky was Zeus who "sometimes shines brightly, sometimes rains."[2] Poseidon was god of the sea, Demeter of growing plants, and so forth. But even those gods whose primary associations were with aspects of human life had much to do with nature as well; indeed, the Greco-Roman traditional religious perspective did not distinguish sharply between human beings and the rest of the natural world. Aphrodite stirred passions not only in human beings, but also in "birds that fly in air and all the many creatures" of land and sea.[3] Among her followers were wolves, lions, bears, and leopards. The music of Apollo's lyre-accompanied voice charmed a "tawny troop of lions" along with "dappled lynxes" and fawns in the mountain forest, causing them all to dance with delight.[4] Asclepius healed by means of snakes. None of the great Greek or Roman gods, and few of the minor ones, lacked identification with elements of the natural environment.

Some were predominately gods of nature. Pan was a watcher of the herds who loved "soft streams," "close thickets," and also "snowy mountains and rocky peaks."[5] He could sometimes offer protection to wild creatures. But the greatest protector of natural things was Artemis, the Roman Diana, the Mistress of Wild Animals (potnia thereon), whose favorite places were "mountains, and forests green, and lonely glades, and sounding rivers,"[6] whose favorite activity was hunting. Let us turn our attention for a while to this goddess and to what she reveals about early attitudes toward hunting as a mode of human relationship to the natural world.

Many of the myths made Artemis something of a game warden; in one variant story, Artemis, or possibly Gē, slew the mighty hunter, Orion, because he boasted that he would kill all animals. Artemis did away with another hunter, Actaeon, by the horribly appropriate method of having his own hounds tear him to bits, ostensibly because he spied on the goddess while she was bathing, but one suspects that there was an earlier version of the myth in which his crime was hunting the sacred deer of Artemis. That is exactly what Sophocles said Agamemnon did to earn his punishment, when "taking his pleasure in her sacred grove, he startled an antlered stag with dappled hide, shot it, and shooting made some careless boast."[7] Artemis demanded the life of Agamemnon's own daughter "in quittance for the wild creature's life." Guthrie calls this incident "perhaps the earliest example of a game preserve,"[8] but I would suggest that divine protection of wildlife is far older than Agamemnon. Artemis was guardian especially of the young of wild animals; she was "gracious to the tender whelps of fierce lions and took delight in the suckling young of every wild creature that roves the field."[9] The cults of Artemis included dances done by children called "bears" or "fawns," probably originally dressed in animal costumes. Here we should emphasize that Artemis's animals are almost exclusively the wild game species that would engage the attention of hunters, not the domestic charges of farmers and herders. The possible exception is the goat, but that creature easily becomes feral, and there were wild goats on most mountains around the Mediterranean.

How can we reconcile with Artemis's protective role the fact that she herself was represented as the huntress par excellence, the "destroyer" who loves hunting wild beasts, accepts the hunters' gifts of wild game, and even holocausts of wild creatures offered to her, as for example in Patrae? How can Artemis, mistress of wild creatures, also be patron goddess of hunters? The apparent contradiction comes from regarding hunter and prey as enemies, a view often expressed by classical writers, to be sure. But preserved in the cults of Artemis and Diana are survivals of earlier attitudes and practices from the time when ancestral societies sustained themselves by hunting, when the animals were seen as powerful beings endowed with spirits like those of human beings, and when hunting was regarded as a "holy occupation" in which both hunter and game animal participated. The hunter was expected to propitiate the animal and to treat it, either alive or dead, with respect. A certain sportsmanlike survival of this earlier functional attitude can be traced in the share of the hunter's bag or fisherman's creel that was offered to Artemis, as well as in Xenophon's remark that "hares below a certain age are left alone as sacred to the goddess."[10] Kenneth Clark sees sacrifice in somewhat the same light: "While men still felt a kinship with animals, to eat them was a crime against the group, and expiation could be achieved only by a ritual feast in which all men were involved."[11] In Greek and Roman sacrifice almost all the meat was eventually consumed by the people. The good hunter, then, who had approached the goddess in respect and observed the proper customs, could expect the kindly permission if not indeed the active aid of the goddess.

But the careful hunter would never intrude on the sacred territories set aside for the gods. Agamemnon's sin, not simply to kill a deer but to do so in a sacred precinct, was avoided by pious Greeks and Romans. Such precincts, called *temenē* in Greek and *templa* in Latin, were areas set aside, usually containing groves of trees and springs or other water, though often mountaintops or other prominent features of topography were so treated. They were very numerous, and within them the environment was preserved in something like its natural state, modified usually only by the addition of an image of the god and perhaps a shrine or temple to protect it. To understand the preservation of groves, we must recall the Greco-Roman attitude toward trees. Classical writers recognized that forests, the groves themselves, were the original temples. Trees were sacred to the gods: the oak to Zeus, the laurel to Apollo, the willow to Hera, the pine tree (or perhaps an oak) to Pan. In fact, trees in general were sacred to the gods; Vergil said that every grove was sacred to Diana. As Pliny explained, "The woods were formerly temples of the deities, and even now simple country folk dedicate a tall tree to a god with the ritual of olden times; and we adore sacred groves and the very silence that reigns in them no less devoutly than images that gleam in gold and ivory."[12]

Stories were told of the protection of trees by the dryads, the spirits whose lives were so closely bound to their trees that to cut one down might kill the nymph who lived in it. Such acts did not go unpunished; Erysichthon, who cut an oak in Ceres' sacred forest, found himself cursed with insatiable hunger as a result of the dryads' complaint. As a punishment for upsetting the balance of nature, hunger seems singularly appropriate.

Protection of sacred groves was not merely matter for myths; Frazer's *Golden Bough* notes a number of cases where cities passed laws forbidding the cutting of trees, removal of wood or leaves, the pasturing of cattle, sheep, or pigs, or planting of grain in sacred groves under penalty of stiff fines, including mandatory sacrifice, and, in one case involving a slave, fifty lashes. Witnesses were required to report the transgressions or suffer similar penalties. The rules of the Arval grove of Dia went so far as to require replacing every tree that fell with a newly planted one. Illegal cultivation of Apollo's sacred land near Delphi was the announced cause of war. To the Greeks and Romans, the sanctity of holy groves was a practical matter in which local ordinances buttressed the retribution of the gods without necessarily replacing it; Cleomenes of Sparta set fire to a sacred grove and was visited by the gods with madness (the fact that five thousand Argives burned to death in that forest fire should also be mentioned).

The practical result of the careful preservation of sacred groves, forbidding even the carrying away of broken limbs in some cases, was the survival of venerable stands of trees after the surrounding areas had been deforested. These were the classical "national parks," small "wilderness areas" surrounded by vast tracts of "clearcutting." Pausanias remarked upon the gigantic size of the trees he saw in these relict forests, some so large as to overshadow hills or to allow people to picnic or sleep in their hollow trunks.

High mountains were also set aside as sacred localities. Sometimes a throne was erected on the summit for Zeus or another deity. The followers of mountain-born Dionysus possibly held that the uplands where they danced in their annual mysteries were set aside for special use. Sometimes a whole island, like Delos, was consecrated as a *temenos*.

Protection within the sacred limits was, as we have already noticed, extended to animals. Generally speaking, hunters were not allowed to go inside with their dogs and weapons. On Mount Lycaeus, if a hunter saw his quarry go into the precinct of Zeus, he had to wait outside, the belief being that if he entered he would die within the year. In places there were deer sacred to Persephone and deer and wild goats sacred to Artemis, none of which could be hunted, although a "special permit" could be issued when a sacrificial victim was desired. There were tortoises on an Arcadian peak and, as Pausanias noted, "the men of the mountain fear to catch them, and will not allow strangers to do so either, for they think they are sacred to Pan."[13] No fishing was allowed in the waters of many sanctuaries, and in some was lawful only for priests. Even eels were sacred in Arethusa.

It would be overstating the case to indicate that precincts were always kept inviolate—no laws would have been necessary if they had been—or that conservation was invariably effective in the hands of the gods. There was an annual Roman festival, the Parilia, in which shepherds were cleansed ritually for trespass in the groves, and Cato records a prayer to be used before cutting down a tree in a sacred grove. Xenophon remarked that men could hire *temenē* from the city of Athens, presumably for some kind of commercial use, and Juvenal complained that foreigners rented groves in Rome.

And what of nature outside the boundaries of the *temenē,* where no special protection was afforded? Greek and Latin writers expressed their admiration for nature through the mouths of the Olympian deities. The subject is too vast to expand upon here, but I cannot resist quoting the Homeric *Hymn to Delian Apollo* as one illustration: "All mountain peaks and high headlands of lofty hills and rivers flowing out to the deep and beaches sloping seaward and havens of the sea are your delight."[14] This certainly implies an Olympian approbation of the entire natural world. But the gods in

Olympian aspect seem more generally to have functioned so as to set the boundaries between the parts of nature that were sacred and those that were not, to lay down the distinctions between what was permitted to mankind and what was not, and to punish those who transgressed the limits. The result was to leave most of nature without divinely sanctioned protection.

Besides the Olympian gods there were the gods of the earth— *chthon*—not the least among whom was Earth herself, great "mother of all, eldest of all beings, who feeds all creatures."[15] She "not only bears the crops for the husbandman, but also the flocks and herds for pastoral peoples, and even the wild creatures whose abundance is necessary for men at a still earlier stage of culture, who live by hunting and fishing."[16] In the chthonic view, all life is sacred because it comes from Mother Earth, herself the greatest deity, and human beings are simply some among her many creatures, animals more like than unlike other animals. Man goes wrong only by getting out of harmony with nature's ways: her cyclical balance, her movements through growth to fruition. Many gods had chthonic aspects, but chthonic religion was always an undercurrent in Greek and Roman thought, seldom emerging above the surface. Had it been the dominant trend, the environmental history of the classical age would have been different. In actuality, the protection afforded to the natural environment by the gods was limited, circumscribed, and often circumvented, particularly as human minds began to throw off the gods' increasingly tenuous hold.

A second set of attitudes we shall consider here is that of the philosophers. A dominant tendency of Greek philosophers and of the Romans who followed in their train was to exclude the gods' actions from their account of nature and also to reify nonhuman nature, setting it apart from mankind as a series of phenomena to be categorized and explained. This approach excluded the participatory sense of identification between human beings and the rest of the natural world which, as noted above, often characterized traditional religious perspectives. But it was not the only posture philosophers could adopt in regard to nature.

I am indebted to John Rodman for an article in which he stressed the importance of another school of philosophers which he calls "a kind of counter-culture," that of Pythagoras and Empedocles, who "exhibited in both theory and practice a deep sense of the kinship of human with nonhuman (especially animal) life."[17] Were these philosophers, these vegetarians, these almost nature-mystics, the early environmentalists we are looking for? This tradition, often called "Orphic" from its quasi-mythical founder, Orpheus, emphasized the harmony of nature and the unity of all living organisms, including human beings, and thus was fundamentally pantheistic. In the view of Empedocles, the universe was an endless recycling of elements in a kind of closed ecosystem: "There is no birth in mortal things, and no end in ruinous death. There is only mingling and interchange of parts, and it is this we call 'nature.' "[18] The idea was echoed by Lucretius: "So the sum of things is constantly renewed, all creatures live in symbiosis [*mutua vivunt*]."[19]

The Orphics and Pythagoreans taught that all living creatures are related and have a common origin and natural ties. The usual iconographic representation of Orpheus shows him surrounded by animals in whom his song has awakened a sympathetic attraction. Pythagoras was said to have charmed an eagle and a bear.

The sense of kinship is supported by the Orphic doctrine that all living creatures, plants as well as animals, have souls like those of human beings and also a kind of intelligence. As Empedocles said, "The soul inhabits every kind of form of animals and plants."[20] There is no scale of values or hierarchy imposed; all creatures are ensouled and participate in the cyclical development of the world. The result of this view was the practice of kindness to other creatures and the refusal to do them harm. Pythagoras taught respect for life, holding that "to kill living beings is contrary to both custom and nature [*anomon kai para physin*]."[21] In the original state of nature, these philosophers held, birds, beasts, and men had been tame and gentle to one another. They urged their followers to abstain from hunting, animal sacrifice, and especially from eating meat. To those who offered animal sacrifice, Empedocles said, "You are sacrificing your own kin."[22] Hunters, butchers, and cooks were to be shunned as tainted by the shedding of blood. Pythagoras also objected to cutting or damaging trees and to eating some kinds of vegetable foods. Living strictly by Orphic principles would have meant a simple, limited diet, but it would not have been impossible. A number of foods, including some staples of the Mediterranean table, could be obtained without destroying animal or vegetable life; Ovid's "Pythagoras" mentioned apples, grapes, milk, and honey as examples.

Of course, one of the motives adduced by the Orphics against taking lives was that the souls of animals and plants are actually the reincarnated souls of human beings. The story of Pythagoras recognizing his departed friend's voice in the howls of a beaten dog has been told too often. But underlying the dogma can be detected a genuine sympathy for nature's creatures in their own right. Pythagoras' soul, it was said, "was constantly passing into whatever plants or animals it pleased."[23] And Empedocles reported, "In the past I have been a boy and a girl, a bush, a bird, and a silent water-dwelling fish."[24] It was noted above that ancestral hunting societies regarded animals as having spirits; Orphism might be in some of its aspects a modified survival of attitudes from those distant times. Dodds, in *The Greeks and the Irrational,* suggested that the Orphic idea of soul-body dualism might have had its origins in the prehistoric hunter-shaman's experiences of "soul-flight," the soul leaving the body, having various experiences, and returning. Perhaps still another element of the old hunters' tribal culture also found its way into Orphism; that is, respect for nonhuman life and reluctance to kill needlessly.

The influence of the tradition of Orpheus, Pythagoras, and Empedocles on environmental thought was, however, not entirely or perhaps even primarily positive, since a salient element was the soul-body dualism mentioned above. The soul was captive in the body, they believed, or in a series of bodies (specifically as a result of the pollution entailed in taking life and eating meat); it was in the soul's best interest to be purified and go free. If this be true, then all bodies, human and nonhuman, are prisons. The world of nature itself must be worse than a prison, indeed, it must be a maze of prisons. Even more seriously, Orphism devalued that portion of the natural environment with which the soul is in closest association, the body itself (as some Pythagoreans put it, *sōma = sēma,* the body is a tomb). The harshness of this view of the body is mitigated elsewhere, as in Empedocles' statement that "mortals can know and recognize" the power of Love in the physical universe, "for she is implanted in their bodies."[25] But one's inescapable impression is that the dualism of soul and body promulgated by this school prepared the way for a crushing indifference to the natural world that became characteristic of much later philosophical religious thought that was touched by it. We will leave Pythagoreanism for now but will return later to see one of its more appealing influences.

In our search for early environmentalists, we might well look at a third set of attitudes to be found in those few outstanding Greek thinkers who originated inquiries we would call ecological. They might be said to have been the forerunners of the science of ecology even though, as is the case with much Greek science, interest in pursuing answers to the kind of questions they were asking did not revive until the modern period.

The philosophical basis of ecology, which conceived the world as a biological system within which cycles of change and interaction occur, was stated by Empedocles in the quotation given above, and repeated here somewhat more fully:

There is no birth in mortal things, and no end in ruinous death. There is only mingling and interchange of parts, and it is this we call 'nature.' . . .
When these elements are mingled into the shape of a man living under the bright sky, or into the shape of wild beasts or plants or birds, men call it birth; and when these things are separated into their parts men speak of hapless death.[26]

One is reminded also of Anaxagoras' statement, "Nothing exists apart; everything has a share of everything else."[27]

Hippocrates investigated the effects of varying natural environments on human health, both physical and mental. He believed that one must understand nature as a whole to understand the human body and soul. According to *Airs, Waters, Places,*[28] the climate, seasons, and winds of a place, the drinking water found there, and the topography and exposure determine to a great extent the physique, temperament, intelligence, and therefore even the culture of the people who live there, along with the characteristic diseases to be expected among them. In addition, he maintained that the same environmental factors affect the growth of domestic and wild animals and plants in each region. Hippocrates' environmental studies were based as far as possible on careful observation of the regions discussed and are not applications a priori of the theory of humors. If ecology is in part the study of how environments affect organisms, then Hippocrates was a pioneer of ecology.

Aristotle, whose "philosophical emphasis is clearly the natural world" and whose "starting point . . . was biology and the notion of organismic development and function,"[29] was interested not only in individual organisms but also in the relationship among living things and between them and the physical environment. In the *Metaphysics,* he said, "All things are ordered together somehow, but not all alike—both fishes and fowls and plants; and the world is not such that one thing has nothing to do with another, but they are connected."[30] This principle clearly makes the study of ecology possible, and Aristotle's own observations on ecological relationships, contained in his biological writings, were so intelligent that he has been given credit for introducing "ecologic considerations into scientific literature," and called the "Father of Animal Ecology."[31]

In the *Historia Animalium,* he notes carefully the preferences of various species in food and competition for food "between such animals as dwell in the same localities or subsist on the same food,"[32] particularly when supplies run short. The lion and civet will compete for meat, and the kite will steal food from the raven. "Thus we see in the creatures above mentioned their mutual friendship or enmity is due to the food they feed on and the life they lead."[33]

Modern ecologists have explained fluctuations of animal populations as resulting from interactions between availability of food, rapidity of reproduction, and predation. Aristotle gave a classic description of a spectacular population increase among mice and subsequent population "crash" in which he noted all the important factors (although he did not attain the complex explanation that would now be regarded as satisfactory). At the beginning of the passage, he described what might be called an experiment in population ecology. A female mouse "in a state of pregnancy was shut up by accident in a vessel containing millet-seed, and after a little while the lid of the vessel was removed and upwards of 120 mice were found inside it."[34] He went on to describe a plague of mice that appeared suddenly, devouring a whole crop. The predators, namely pigs, foxes, and ferrets, were active but ineffective in thinning the numbers, until a rapid disappearance of the mice "after heavy rains."

Other ecological relationships described by Aristotle include territoriality among mammals and birds and animal behavior such as competition and dominance within species, migration, and hibernation. Symbiosis, including parisitism and commensalism, is discussed by means of several examples including the noted one of the sea creature called the pinna and a small crab, the "pinna-guard." "If the pinna be deprived of this pinna-guard," he said, "it soon dies."[35]

Aristotle's systematic view of nature, however, falls short of being ecological in the scientific sense. His scheme is hierarchical and pyramidal. Although each level of nature intergrades into the next so that sharp distinctions between classes are difficult, for example, "in most of the other animals can be discerned traces of the psychical modes which attain their clearest differentiation in man,"[36] still "there is one ultimate ruler, and each lower level is subordinate to the next higher level, as in an army."[37] Anthony Preus, in a very useful discussion of Aristotle's biological writings, uses a political analogy, calling Aristotle's ecology "aristocratic." As Preus points out, Aristotle in the *Politics* "argues not only for natural slavery, but also that plants exist 'for the sake of' animals, and animals exist 'for the sake of' man."[38] But scientific ecology sees nature as a reticulum, a web or net of complex interrelationships that are neither hierarchical, pyramidal, nor aristocratic. Scientific ecology sees the existence of each species as depending upon and supporting a series of interactions with other species and nonliving components of the environment. In such a view, questions as to whether one species is "more valuable" than another can only be answered in terms relative to a particular problem chosen for study.[39] Any system that imposes a structure of values a priori will inevitably distort the network of relationships discovered and described by scientific ecology. Aristotle's ecology is therefore unscientific insofar as it is "aristocratic," whether its apex value is man or something beyond man.

Theophrastus, the student of Aristotle who extended his teacher's researches into botany, adopted an ecological model that was more "democratic" than Aristotle's. When Theophrastus looked for the purpose (*telos*) of a plant, he found it in the production of seeds for the perpetuation of the same species, not in producing food for animals or man. He was interested in efficient causes, not in final causes, and thus much closer to the spirit of modern science. As he expressed it in his *Metaphysics*, "We must try to find a certain limit . . . both to 'final causation' and to the 'impulse to the better.' " For this is the beginning of the inquiry about the universe, that is, of the effort to determine "the conditions on which real things depend and the relations in which they stand to one another."[40] Since he was also a careful observer of nature, he was able to provide ecological explanations of many natural phenomena.

He stressed the importance of observing plants both in undisturbed ecosystems (since where a plant grows unaided best reveals the environment to which it is best adapted) and under cultivation (which he holds to be an environmental change that operates in fundamentally natural ways). He speculated on the interplay between the "tendency of the plant's nature" (which would today be called "genotype") and the environment, giving importance to both.

We would call much of Theophrastus' writings a botanical *Airs, Waters, Places,* if by that we mean that he considers these environmental factors and do not impute to him quite as ardent a belief in environmental determinism as Hippocrates expressed. Theophrastus noted the influences of long-term climate, the growing season, and short-term changes in the weather, including temperature, wind, and rain, on the distribution and growth habits of plants. He observed the effects of changes in climate brought about by changes in the size and location of bodies of water due to natural or human agency. He distinguished among plants adapted to conditions of aridity (xerophytes), moisture (hydrophytes), and salinity (halophytes), and to various types of soil. He provided extensive discussion of the effects of slope, exposure to wind and sun, and elevation on environmental conditions in small areas (microclimates) and the plants that grow in them, and he noted correctly that mountains provide an unusual variety of these. He saw that plants of limited distribution (narrow endemics) can be associated with particular mountains or isolated marshes.

Theophrastus used certain classifying terms that are still important to ecologists; for example, he distinguished among trees, shrubs, and undershrubs. He knew that plants compete with each other for food, water, and sunlight, and he distinguished between shade-tolerant and shade-intolerant trees. He described the spread of weeds and cases of symbiosis and parisitism. He understood that legumes enrich the soil and that decomposing leaves can provide a seedbed.

The interaction between animals and plants, through grazing and other means, received his attention. Insects, he pointed out, are often species-specific or limited to certain regions, and some plants have odors that repel them. Cultivation and other human interactions with plants form a major theme. He knew that human beings affect plants in positive and negative ways, on the one hand through manuring and other forms of tendance and on the other hand through burning, cutting, and even the trampling of armies. He recorded regulations governing the harvest of wild plants and the felling of trees and had heard that the cedars of Lebanon grew to great size where they were protected in "paradises" under Persian supervision.

Since, as noted above, Aristotle has been called the "Father of Animal Ecology," it might be plausible to distinguish Theophrastus as "Father of Plant Ecology." But while Aristotle provided us with a few outstanding descriptions and insights, Theophrastus adopted a consistent ecological viewpoint supported by observations of greater extent, variety, and importance. His philosophical stance is more congenial to ecological discoveries. Theophrastus is clearly the most important early ecologist.

Unfortunately, these Greek forerunners of scientific ecology had few followers. No ancient thinkers expanded on their ecological contributions, and they cannot be shown to have had any effect on practice. In medieval times, Theophrastus was known only as the author of the satirical *Characters,* and Aristotle's biological writings were generally ignored in favor of the *Politics* and *Ethics*.

Fourth and last, let us consider the attitudes of those who might loosely be called the ancient world's environmental protest movement. There were a number of Greek and Roman writers who recognized some environmental problems caused by human beings. A few of them went so far as to speak out against the practices that caused the problems and to advocate their elimination.

Vitruvius, the Roman architect, was aware of water pollution caused by mining and the resulting danger to health. He advised methods of testing water for purity and particularly warned against lead pipes as a source of contamination harmful to the human body. He also described lead poisoning caused by industrial air pollution: "We can take example by the workers in lead who have complexions affected by pallor. For when, in casting, the lead receives the current of air, the fumes from it occupy the members of the body, and burning them thereupon, rob the limbs of the virtue of the blood."[41] He further suggested a method of testing air in mines for dangerous pollutants.

Strabo, the geographer, also observed industrial air pollution. In Iberia, he noted, "They build their silver-smelting furnaces with high chimneys, so that the gas from the ore may be carried high into the air, for it is heavy and deadly."[42]

Soil erosion due to deforestation was described by Plato in a noted passage in the *Critias.* That the soil had become increasingly exhausted since earlier, better days was a commonplace among Greek and Roman agricultural writers. Lucretius and others believed this was inevitable, as Mother Earth was growing old, but more practical farmers, such as Xenophon and Columella blamed the neglect of careless human beings: "Land, as all men know, responds to good treatment."[43] Horace scorned "the owner contemptuous of the land."[44] The major role of goats in destroying trees and other vegetation was noted by Varro.

But the urban environment received the most graphic criticism, at least during the Roman period. "The smoke, the wealth, the noise of Rome,"[45] repelled Horace, who also objected to the city's suburban encroachment on fertile farmlands. Martial catalogued the many sources of sleep-preventing noise pollution in Rome, including traffic, hammers, and loud schoolteachers. Juvenal expanded the list of urban ills, decrying traffic congestion, fires, public works projects that destroyed natural beauty, chamber pots emptied out upper story windows, and ever increasing crime and vandalism. Seneca joined him in criticizing the "towering tenements, so dangerous to the persons who dwell in them"[46] through imminent collapse.

The polarity between city and country provided a major theme in Greek and Latin literature, and the comparison was almost always favorable to the country. From Theocritus on, writers glorified pastoral and bucolic life as closer to nature and therefore to be preferred. Dio Chrysostom devoted his *Euboean Discourse* to a demonstration of the moral superiority of a hunter's clan to town dwellers. Those who shared such a view of the urban and rural environments might well be expected to "protest with their feet" by leaving the city and to advise others to do the same. Horace, Martial, Juvenal, and others did just that, in the firm conviction that in so doing they were not simply shunning human society (as Heraclitus and Menander's title character in the *Dyscolus* had done by retiring into the mountains) but were enabling themselves to choose their company more wisely and giving themselves enough living space to recover their essential humanity. "There's no place in the city for a poor man to get a little peace and a chance to talk."[47]

Another line of protest represented the survival of some of the Pythagorean ideas discussed above. Maintaining the sanctity of all life and the possession of rational souls by animals, some writers in the Roman period objected to hunting, a meat diet, animal sacrifice, and the slaughters for public entertainment in the arenas. Pythagoras himself was given a voice in Ovid's *Metamorphoses*, where he advised King Numa against animal food, since it is through eating the flesh of living creatures that the Golden Age came to an end, and against animal sacrifice as making the very gods the partners of men in wickedness.

Plutarch also voiced Pythagorean protest. In his dialogue, *Whether Land or Sea Animals are Cleverer*, ostensibly a learned debate among cultured huntsmen, Plutarch actually argues that animals possess reason to support his contention. He admits that animals have only a degree of reason but notes that this is also true of human beings. If what we want is "true reason and wisdom, not even man may be said to exercise it."[48] But if animals are rational, then we are unjust to kill them when they have not injured us. Plutarch is not fully a Pythagorean; he denies plants souls, and elsewhere he would permit killing animals "in pity and sorrow,"[49] as well as eating meat as an unfortunate necessity.

But Plutarch's most delightful word on the subject is a brief dialogue between Odysseus, Gryllus, and Circe. Circe, the witch, had changed many men into beasts of various kinds. Odysseus won the right to have his own sailors re-transformed and then asked Circe to release the other Greeks from their animal forms. Circe agreed on one condition: that Odysseus convince a spokesman for the beasts to return willingly to human form. The one chosen to speak for the animals was Gryllus, a hog granted the power of speech by Circe. Gryllus refused the chance to return to human form, since animals, he maintained, are superior to mankind in every virtue; courage, temperance, and intelligence. Moreover, animal virtues are natural; humans must cultivate theirs. Odysseus, the famous persuasive arguer, lost the contest. Having maintained that beasts cannot be rational if they have no inborn knowledge of God, he was reminded by Gryllus that his own father was Sisyphus, a famous atheist. That Plutarch's clever dialogue was not just a set piece is evident from his serious objections voiced elsewhere to hunting, animal slaughter, and the excesses of the Roman arena. Plutarch, rejecting the argument of Hesiod and the Stoics that "human beings have no compact of justice with irrational animals,"[50] exhibited admiration and sympathy for the myriad forms of living things and was an early defender of animal rights.[51]

In society today, we can identify groups and individuals whose ideas and efforts are analogous to the sets of attitudes here studied. It is a sobering observation that none of the Greeks and Romans we have mentioned, whether the approaches they adopted were religious, philosophical, scientific, or literary, were markedly successful in preventing the environmental deterioration of the Mediterranean basin in classical times.

CHAPTER FOUR

Ecological Crisis and Response in Ancient China

by Lester J. Bilsky

At first consideration, the title of this essay may seem particularly sterile for the modern Western reader. Surely, only antiquarians of an antisocial bent could be interested in rehashing events that took place over two thousand years ago in a civilization which developed independently of the Western world and which contributed only marginally to the Western way of life.

First impressions can be misleading, however. In spite of the gaps in time and distance which separate ancient China from the modern West, some close parallels exist between the two. The modern history of the West, emerging from what we identify as the Middle Ages, has witnessed a rising population and significant changes in social organization, the latter related to the growth of business and an urban middle class. Numerous states have developed as independent, nationalistic entities but have nevertheless remained tied to each other in a multi-state system featuring shifting alliances punctuated by occasional conflicts as the states have sought either to protect themselves from their neighbors or to gain advantage over them.

In the recent past, Western ideals and modes of life have penetrated the entire world, where all nations have become enmeshed in the legal, diplomatic, and military maneuverings of the multi-state system. The growth in the scale of our activities, as more people have come to expect higher standards of living, and the growth in international competition and tensions have all led to severe pressures on our natural environment. We are presently concerned with the availability of the natural resources upon which we depend. We are threatened with an ecological crisis, a state in which the economic, social, and political systems adapted to our present environment may break down in the face of significant changes in environmental conditions.

China, during a period from about the eighth century through the third century B.C., can be described in remai..ably similar terms. No census records exist from that early period, but there are indisputable signs of a growing population and of social changes associated with the emergence of business communities. New cities were built in great number. Markets and trade became matters of importance in the writings of the period, and the expansion of trade was further evidenced by an increasing use of coinage. An early, hereditary aristocracy started being displaced by an aristocracy of talent, a group of men whose access to power derived from education received in new schools open to any who could afford the tuition. Officials serving the Chinese states needed considerable training in order to handle the burgeoning complexities of political management. Among their skills they needed to know the niceties of diplomatic procedure involved in the operation of a multi-state system which developed to encompass the entire civilized world known to the Chinese.

Population growth, economic development and the need for military preparedness in states whose rivalries overshadowed the temporary accomodations of diplomatic alliances all put increasing pressure on the states' natural resources. From the seventh century B.C. on, occasional reports of isolated famines appear in Chinese records. In the fourth century B.C., it is apparent that famine in many areas had reached crisis proportions. In one state, for example, the people were in a condition where "in good years, their lives are continually embittered, and, in bad years, they do not escape perishing."[1] Elsewhere, "in bad calamitous years, and years of famine, the old and feeble . . . who have been found lying in the ditches and water-channels, and the able-bodied, who have been scattered about to the four quarters, have amounted to several thousand."[2] Crisis conditions were not stemmed until widespread social, economic and political adjustments occurred in the Chinese world.

The Chinese, then, in a period of development similar in many ways to our own, fell prey to the same kind of ecological crisis that threatens us. One of the major differences between the two periods, of course, is that China's crisis occurred two thousand years ago. The Chinese have left enough historical records, however, to give us a basis for reconstructing what caused their crisis and what steps they took to deal with it. The purpose of this chapter is to examine this historical evidence from China and analyze it in the light of modern studies. Since ancient China's ecological crisis represents a completed case which we can view in its totality, we can hope that its analysis will shed new light on our present concerns and give us an understanding of possible ramifications for our own future.

Contemporary demographers, faced with the problem of a mounting population, have made systematic studies of population response to environmental pressures. A measure of the equivalence of past and present problems is found in the observation of contemporary population historians that early Chinese writers used ideas which are only now being restated. As one work on demography puts it, the Chinese were concerned with concepts of optimum population and of checks to population growth. They "postulated an ideal proportion between land and population, any major deviation from which would create poverty. They held the government primarily responsible for maintaining such a proportion. . . . They observed that mortality increases when the food supply is insufficient."[3]

Equivalence, of course, means that just as Chinese observations make sense at present, our own views should apply to the past. If we look to the models our natural and social scientists have developed in their effort to understand current ecological and demographic problems, we can find organized approaches to help us integrate and analyze scattered, unrelated historical data. Furthermore, when such models are applied to an historical situation with a known outcome, the correctness with which they measure that outcome provides an otherwise unobtainable confirmation of their validity.

A basic starting point for current models is the postulate that a society's standard of living is dependent on the interrelationships of its population level, its environment, the technology available to it and the way in which it is organized. One of the best models for our purpose which embodies this postulate is contained in Alfred Sauvy's *General Theory of Population*. In figure 1.5 of Professor Boughey's essay (p. 23) we see the key relationships in Sauvy's formulation. P represents population, Q is the subsistence requirement for an individual and marginal output is the increase in productivity gained by adding one person to the previous total output of a population. Other conditions remaining equal, the figure indicates that as a population increases, it passes through several successive positions: the maximum marginal productivity, or fastest rate in total growth; M_eP_e, the maximum standard of living or economic optimum; M_pP_p, the maximum of power or the power optimum, where the marginal output reaches the subsistence level; and M_mP_m, the maximum possible population, when the standard of living reaches the subsistence level. Technological improvements can raise the standard of living and, thus, the respective maximums, without otherwise affecting their relationship on the curve.

None of the maximums should be taken as precise points capable of numerical measurement in any given society. Our knowledge of factors contributing to optimum conditions is not yet so precise. It is the positions of the maximums on the curves and the interpretations we derive from them that count for us. The power and economic maximums are the points of greatest interest.

The power optimum represents that point at which a population's primary producers, largely farmers in an agricultural society like China's, put out the maximum quantity of materials to support such nonproducers as rulers, officials and soldiers.

Public authorities acquire material power by levying a certain amount of wealth off each man's output. To get the greatest possible power with a given population, everything above the subsistence level should be levied, leaving each with just enough to live and work, and spending the rest of the resources on the aim pursued (armament, for instance) . . . [After the power optimum has been reached], any extra inhabitant . . . not producing enough supplies for himself, would not be useful since he would need part of the output of the others to feed him, thus diminishing the power of the group.[4]

In an agrarian society in which farmers are subject to a levy, their interest lies in increasing their numbers in order to share out the tax burden. Their increase continues until they are forced to develop sub-marginal land, while their ruler's exactions are limited only by the onset of such conditions as famine, excessive mortality or by the escape of productive workers into beggary, banditry or to another realm through emigration.

According to a more detailed analysis of agrarian societies presented in Ester Boserup's *The Conditions of Agricultural Growth,* while the society as a whole may become overpopulated, a ruler who siphons off too many people as servants and soldiers and taxes the remainder too heavily causes rural underpopulation relative to the total population. In such a condition, the farmers produce too little food, too much of which is taxed away. Insufficient stocks are retained to tide the farmers over years of bad harvest. Given sufficient pressure, members of the village population will have to escape or die. Famine and death do not remedy the population pressure, however, for as Sauvy points out a ruler tends to preserve his power by encouraging his subjects to restore their numbers.

The development of a middle class exacerbates the problems of an agrarian state. Mercantile and manufacturing activities may seem desirable, inasmuch as they create new products, wealth and comfort for a ruler and his people. But the basic goal of the middle class is to maximize its standard of living by increasing its own wealth. In doing so, it both competes with a ruler for primary producers' goods and creates conditions favoring population reduction. Its interests, tending towards the economic optimum, inevitably must clash with those of a ruler whose goal is to increase population to achieve the power optimum. If such a ruler is to maintain his authority, he must take steps to bring middle-class activities under control.

We must now apply the data that survive from ancient China to the theoretical construct described above. We have already considered reports of famine and emigration during the period we are dealing with. The initial explanation advanced by the Chinese for these effects and the popular common sense view taken by most people since is that food shortages must result from natural disasters: the floods, droughts, plagues of insects and the like which cause crops to fail. The model presented here, however, points to the less direct but no less important factors of population size in relationship to food production, taxation and overall state expenditures.

The Chinese, unfortunately, have not left us the figures we should like to have about population size and fluctuations or about food production and caloric intake per person. A few notices about taxation levels have been transmitted, but being discontinuous and divorced from specific population and production amounts they are of limited use. We do, however, have what seems to be fairly complete accounts of the warfare that occurred during our period. It is clear that warfare disrupts normal farming by taking men away from their fields and by destroying crop lands during the course of battle. We can hypothesize further that, during a period in which fighting was frequent, military expenses were not only a major portion of a state's budget but also were subject to greater fluctuations than other budgetary items. An increase in warfare, then, would tend both to decrease production and increase the tax burden a ruler imposed on his subjects. Regardless of the absolute population an area might support at any given time, we can infer that a territory depleted of manpower and material reserves in time of war would be barely able to support even fewer people than the number who could obtain adequate livings in it in times of peace. A natural disaster in such a situation would depress the carrying capacity of the territory still further.

The period from the eighth through the third century B.C., the age of the Eastern Chou dynasty, can be subdivided on the basis of different groups of texts into two parts, a Ch'un Ch'iu (Spring and Autumn) era from 722-475 B.C. and a Chan Kuo (Warring States) era from 474-222 B.C. An analysis of the incidence of warfare, natural disasters and famines during the former era indicates that natural disasters were relatively constant throughout the era. Four to seven of them occurred in each quarter century, enough to trigger famines at any time. The famines, however, are closely related to the incidence of warfare. When warfare among the Chinese states reached peaks of intensity, so too did famines, after a lag of a few years. This time lag is to be expected, for it takes time before the effects of military expenditures mount to the point where acute distress is suffered and where natural disasters can reduce production below the level needed to sustain a population. It also takes time for cuts in military spending to begin to improve general conditions of life. Thus famines tended to reach their peak after the states discovered they could no longer sustain high levels of warfare and had already cut back on their military activities.

Warfare first rose in intensity in the late seventh century. The rulers of China's states were forced at that time to come to grips with some of the economic realities controlling their situation. The first recourse of rulers faced with increased expenses was, naturally enough, to raise new revenues. The earliest reports of systematic taxation appear in records from the beginning of the sixth century B.C. Interestingly enough, a famine, triggered by a plague of locusts, followed only months after the first tax collection in one state. Farmers at the time, whether because of mounting numbers or increasing economic pressures, were apparently encroaching on wooded areas where game was still to be found. As a result, we also find reports of forest lands being enclosed as rulers' parks or hunting preserves. It would seem that rulers, in this early stage of economic shortage had yet to decide whether to retain their traditional habits of life or to abandon the past in favor of behavior more pertinent to their problems.

In spite of the love rulers had for conserving tradition and pursuing pleasures, the time came when such things were luxuries too expensive to be retained. A ruler was as bound to his subjects as they were to him. If he caused too much deprivation, his subjects eventually must die, rebel or flee, leaving him with nothing. He had only two possible ways to prevent such calamities. He could reduce his expenditures, or increase his subjects' capacity to pay his levies, or both. To accomplish the first, he could either cut back on programs which absorbed his revenues or he could improve the efficiency of his administration, making his funds go further. An increase in state revenues could be achieved in several ways: by limiting the ability of the middle class to siphon off funds from the state, by encouraging technological developments which increased individual output and, most effectively, by investing in projects designed to return future production dividends.

We find China's rulers undertaking all of these courses of action by the second half of the sixth century B.C. A general truce was negotiated among Chinese states in 546 B.C. Even when fighting broke out again in 538, it remained at low levels for at least half a century. The decline in warfare was followed by a temporary abatement of famine conditions.

Simultaneously, states adopted new bureaucratic procedures which endowed their governments with greater power and increased efficiency. Many new offices were created to deal directly with state revenues and the preservation of natural resources. Fields and wild areas were surveyed, new forms of tax registries created and officials appointed to supervise use of forests, lakes, coastal areas and the like. Other officials imposed some restraints on trade by supervising market transactions. Eventually, some of the Chinese states began to take direct control over business activities and profits through creating state-run monopolies in such commodities as salt and iron. Other states, not possessing lucrative resources of this sort, simply undertook to force people out of business and back to the land, where they could farm and produce hearty sons to be drafted into public labor projects and military service.

The need to expand bureaucracies created a corresponding need to seek men with specific, advanced training to staff offices. State-sponsored academies and private schools both came into existence. From these emerged the "Hundred Schools of Thought," the famous early Chinese systems of philosophy. While some teachings were oriented toward such technical subjects as laws, bureaucratic organization and agricultural practices, others delved deeply into general social and political questions. They advocated solutions ranging from the total abandonment of the complexity and waste of large-scale social organization to the imposition of strict political order on all human actions, concepts which would eventually be applied to environmental issues. The schools' students, well prepared to make innovative approaches to the problems faced by the governments of their time, developed and then refined the new bureaucratic measures described above.

China's early schools were deeply involved in the social changes that marked the period. By encouraging or discouraging different types of livelihood, state bureaucratic systems developed increasing control over individuals' social and economic advancement. States conferred power, wealth and status on their officials. Officials even had a fair degree of security, despite the grave peril of incurring a ruler's displeasure. Once states discovered the need to recruit the talented, any individual, even the scion of a hereditary aristocratic house, had to seek special training to qualify for an official position. The sons of middle class families, finding business limited more and more by official restraints, also tended to pursue bureaucratic careers by entering schools. Such students, having gained means of fulfilling high ambitions and having transferred their loyalties from their families to their states, acquiesced in policies that subordinated individual rights to the needs of the states. Thus, the very existence of state bureaucracies backed by open education imposed conditions which effectively eliminated the old aristocracy and stunted the development of middle-class power but perpetuated bureaucratic organization and authority.

State bureaucracies gave rulers the organizational capability of channeling investment funds into major development projects. In the late sixth and early fifth centuries B.C., a rash of irrigation and transport canal construction occurred. As one source puts it, in addition to several major canals, "there were literally millions of smaller canals which led off from the larger ones at numerous points along their courses and were employed to irrigate an increasingly large area of land."[5] It was clearly recognized that these canals brought much new wealth to the areas in which they were built.

Agricultural output was also spurred by the adoption of fallowing and manuring techniques and by the increasing use of labor-saving bronze and cast iron tools—spades, picks, hoes, rakes, sickles, axes and plows. Although the iron plowshare was a thin, fragile sheath fitted over a wooden base and was set at too wide an angle to bite deeply into the soil, it made possible the development of an ox-drawn plow, adding an important new energy source to supplement human labor.

All of these new technological, social and political developments, however, did not prove sufficient to remedy permanently the difficulties of the Chinese states. While the standard of living must have risen for a time in many areas, new problems appeared and underlying problems remained. The new technology had its drawbacks as well as its benefits. The more iron that was smelted, the more wood that had to be cut and burned to make charcoal. The more wood that was cut, the greater the danger of soil erosion from hillsides stripped of their forests. Furthermore, much of China's additional production had to be spread among a growing population, while part tended to be soaked up by rulers' increased expenditures on lavish new palaces, temples, tombs and personal pleasures.

Most serious of all was the continued existence of rivalries among states. Patterns of warfare changed in the fifth century B.C. Numerous small states were swallowed up by their larger neighbors, leaving a handful of Chinese "super-powers" to compete for supremacy. The increased use of bronze and the introduction of iron provided the surviving states with new quantities of weapons as well as new farming tools. The number of wars fought diminished, but each war tended to be longer and involved hundreds of thousands, instead of tens of thousands, of troops. Military expenses must have gone up enormously, while investment funds had to be diverted from productive projects to the construction of defensive works such as the long walls erected along state borders, walls that made up the bulk of the late third century B.C. Great Wall.

Sources of the Chan Kuo era show the incidence of warfare escalating to a new peak in the second quarter of the fourth century B.C., followed by an abrupt decline and finally a return to an intermediate, sustainable level. Unfortunately, we do not have correspondingly accurate data during this era for natural disasters and famines. If the relationships hypothesized earlier hold, however, the data suggest that economic distress and famines should have reached a new peak by the third quarter of the fourth century, continuing at less acute but still serious levels through the end of the era. In fact, it is in the fourth century B.C. that Chinese writers first go beyond their earlier practice of merely making routine mention of famines. They begin to dwell on the sufferings of the common people caused by famine. Struck by the grim reality of crisis conditions, they look for causes and find a close relationship between dearth and war. As one source puts it,

When the sound of war is heard, personal wealth must be diminished to make soldiers wealthy; food and drink are rationed to pamper suicide warriors; carriages are smashed to make firewood; and oxen are slaughtered to feast the armies. This is the way to collapse and ruin. . . . [After battle] families of the dead impoverish themselves to bury their kin; households of the wounded exhaust their wealth to get them medicines, while those left sound drink so heavily and spend so wildly that as much is wasted by them as is spent on the dead and wounded. In the end the people will have spent more than can be restored in ten years of harvests.[6]

The ecological crisis conditions that persisted after the fourth century B.C. helped to tilt the balance of power in China. The state of Ch'in, which had been one of China's more remote and underdeveloped lands before the onset of acute environmental crisis, took advantage of the difficulties arising in other states in the fourth century while concentrating its resources on internal development. Instead of sinking men and money into the central Chinese battleground, Ch'in conquered vast new territories and turned them into fertile sources of wealth and power. Immigrants who fled impossible conditions elsewhere came and put the new lands into production. Ch'in's officials imposed strict bureaucratic regimes which severely limited business and encouraged agricultural production. In the early third century B.C., the investment of large sums for the construction of two immense irrigation systems made more land available for settlement and generated even more revenue. Ch'in applied large portions of its newly developed wealth to build China's most powerful army and, in the 230s and 220s, used its forces to conquer all of its rival states.

Ch'in's creation of a unified empire was the step that brought China's ecological crisis under control. Ch'in imperial rule lasted but a dozen years. Its successor state, however, the former Han dynasty, built a reign of two hundred years on the base established by the Ch'in and bequeathed its traditions of government to the dynasties which succeeded it during the next two thousand years. Imperial government created little that was new. Its success lay in consolidating and organizing the programs innovated by the warring states of the pre-imperial era. Unification alone helped by reducing the need for maintaining armies as large as in pre-imperial times and by calming the internal upheavals caused by internecine warfare. The by-products of unification were many. A single bureaucracy replaced many, lowering government costs, at least initially, by a reduction in personnel. Greater efficiency and cost-effectiveness were achieved through the establishment of nationwide policies: a unified currency, one set of trade transport regulations, common standards for official training and appointments, for control of natural resources, operation of grain storehouses for disaster relief and so on. Vast construction programs were planned and completed on the basis of the nation's greatest needs. Underlying all these measures was the establishment of an imperial ideological system which gave divine sanction to the emperor's unique right to regulate the social status and activities of all Chinese, to subordinate individual freedom of action to the common good. In sum, by approaching more nearly than the earlier Chinese states could the theoretical goal of keeping as many people as possible in primary production roles and reconciling them to near subsistence conditions of life, the empire was generally able to reduce ecological pressures to bearable levels.

Having looked at the case history of ancient China's ecological crisis, we should once again turn to the question of how that experience applies to the contemporary scene. We began by considering a number of similar conditions. It will be well also to take some differences into account. Unlike China's agricultural society, the West has an urban, industrialized culture. We have developed one technological innovation after another to raise our productivity to ever higher levels. Unfortunately, much as the Chinese outgrew their technical advances, we also seem to have come near the limits of any known technological solutions to the mounting problems of our day. The most comprehensive current models indicate that world ecological collapse will occur before the year 2100 unless technology is supplemented by social controls.

Again unlike China, Western society is predominately middle class, valuing a tradition of democratic rule and individual freedom. We must wonder, however, if individual rights can be maintained against the growth of government controls brought on by social and environmental pressures.

It is certain that, the differences being what they are, the West will not duplicate the early Chinese historical example. And yet, it is interesting to note that the United States civil service examination system has been borrowed from the Chinese examinations innovated in early imperial times, that the New Deal based its farm price support system on China's early imperial "Ever-Normal Granary," and that our bureaucratic agencies and commissions have proliferated, even as the Chinese did, to regulate products, trade and use of our environment. It may be well for us to keep the Chinese example in mind.

PART THREE

THE ECOLOGY OF THE EUROPEAN MIDDLE AGES

Introduction

by Thomas E. Kaiser

   Medieval Europe provides the historian of ecological crises with a splendid field for research. Sufficiently remote in time to permit the historian to view developments in a wide historical perspective, the Middle Ages have left an historical record sufficiently rich in documents to allow for meaningful conclusions about the medieval environment. Inspired by the ground-breaking work of Marc Bloch, medievalists have established a firmly rooted tradition of inquiry into the ecology of the Middle Ages which gives the present-day historian of the period a special advantage and which has provided all the contributors to this section with a foundation to build upon.

   The following essays offer the reader a number of approaches to the ecological history of medieval Europe; together they illuminate not only the "objective" environmental conditions of the age but also the "subjective" human perceptions of the environment (which, of course, helped to define the "objective" conditions). Professor Lewis analyzes the ecology of seven critical regions worthy of special attention because their importance was new to the Middle Ages. Professor Bowlus investigates the ecology of the high and late Middle Ages when both "objective" conditions and "subjective" perceptions underwent monumental change. Professor Herlihy defines four major sets of attitudes toward nature held by the men of the Middle Ages which conditioned human expectations and practices.

These papers shed light on a number of topics whose implications can be fully understood only when historians use a general ecological approach to them. Such a topic is medieval timber resources and the forests from which they came. Professor Lewis demonstrates how the availability of wood affected the dynamics of the maritime history of lands in the Mediterranean area during the early Middle Ages and of the North Sea region during the late Middle Ages. Professor Bowlus comments on the central role of timber resources in the economic and demographic expansion of the eleventh, twelfth, and thirteenth centuries. Wood, he shows, was both an essential building material and a significant energy source, necessary for a wide variety of social enterprises, from the smelting of iron tools of war to the building of the Gothic cathedrals, the quintessential expression of the medieval spirit. The decreasing supply of wood seems to have played a crucial role in bringing about the most serious economic contraction Europe experienced since the decline of the Roman empire in the West. Professor Herlihy, taking a slightly different approach, discusses timber with regard to the changing perception of man's relationship to nature as a whole; the timber resources of Europe, at first in their depleted state a symbol of the bareness of the natural world and the vanity of this worldly existence, became the embodiment in turn of man's fear of the unknown, of his sense of worldly mastery, and finally of his search for recreation and inner peace. From their various standpoints these authors show how human attitudes can be shaped by natural ecological forces, for example, how the encroaching forests of the early medieval period reinforced man's notion of nature as an antagonist—and how human attitudes can affect the balance of natural forces—how man's belief in his ability to utilize natural resources during the later Middle Ages helped to produce massive deforestation.

To attempt to draw from these three essays any firm conclusions regarding the most controversial issues of medieval ecological history—the influence of climatological shifts, the origins of the revival of the eleventh century, the degree to which the fourteenth-century ecological crisis was a product of Malthusian forces—would be ill advised, for historians must conduct far more research on these matters before any such conclusions can be confirmed or refuted. Yet these papers do lend weight to certain conceptions of the medieval past. First, they suggest that within the thousand years of medieval history there existed a variety of ecological systems whose differences were marked. There was no single medieval environment, no single medieval attitude toward nature, but rather a complex pattern of interactions between the natural and social worlds which shifted considerably over the period 500 to 1500 A.D., indeed, which shifted as dramatically within that time span as it has since then. Second, the articles reveal a record of creative response to ecological problems that belies the idea, still widely held, that the Middle Ages was an age of technological and economic stagnation. Professor Lewis demonstrates how many new geographical regions were exploited by medieval man, while Professor Bowlus gives us a view of a sustained medieval economic expansion that cannot fail to impress even students of modern industrial revolutions. When one considers in addition to these developments the later medieval transformation of attitudes toward nature that Professor Herlihy describes, transformations without which the modern scientific movement might never have occurred, the achievement of medieval civilization comes to appear all the more imposing. Finally, the essays portray an episode in ecological history with a structure similar to that of the modern age. After a period of economic contraction, a period of roughly two centuries follows which is characterized by more or less uninterrupted economic expansion and population growth tied to an intensifying exploitation of natural resources. Subsequently, there begins a period of increasing strain on productive capacities coupled with a progressive exhaustion of raw materials. The strain on productive capacities places strain on the culture as a whole, leading to a re-examination of human expectations of the future in particular and the whole range of human values in general. Whether the coming ecological crisis of our own age will produce a catastrophe as severe as that of the Black Death or be followed by cultural movements of such brilliance as the Renaissance and the Scientific Revolution are concerns which can only arouse our most profound fears and hopes.

CHAPTER FIVE

Ecology and the Sea
in Medieval Times (300-1500 A.D.)

by Archibald R. Lewis

This chapter will deal with ecology and the sea in seven maritime areas of Europe and North Africa during the Middle Ages. These have been chosen not only because they represent the most vital areas during these centuries but also because theirs was a *new* importance since classical times. They are as follows: the Bosphorus-Hellespont region between the Black Sea and the Aegean, the upper Adriatic, the western Mediterranean from the Tiber to the Ebro, both shores of the Straits of Gibraltar, the eastern English Channel and the southern North Sea near the Straits of Dover, the west coast of Norway near Bergen, and the Kattegat-Skagerrak region between Norway, Denmark, and Sweden. All of these maritime regions, incidentally, are still of vital importance to European trade and economic life.

Although it would be possible to examine each of them in a number of ecological contexts, only three vital elements will be considered here: timber supplies for ship construction, fish of commercial importance, and salt in large quantities. It is hoped thus to throw light on how medieval man was affected by ecological considerations long before Rachel Carson and others began to focus their attention on the sea's role in the ecological balance of modern civilization.

Before considering each of these maritime areas in detail, however, a few overall comments are in order, especially as regards the initial period between 300 and 750 A.D. First, let us look at climatic changes. There seems to be a general agreement among climatologists that the early Middle Ages were significantly warmer than today. Then, from the eighth century on, winters gradually grew colder, until by the late 1400s Europe entered a period sometimes called the "Little Ice Age." It does not appear, however, that these climatic changes had much ecological effect upon the elements concerning us—timber resources, fish supplies, or salt production.

More crucially, these early medieval centuries saw a general population decline in both the Roman and non-Roman worlds. This decline began in the third century, continued through the fourth and fifth, especially in the West, and reached its apogee in the sixth and seventh when both the Mediterranean world and the area of the Northern Seas were wracked by bubonic plague originating in the Far East. This steady and almost inexorable decline in population helped to end urban life and organized agricultural villas in lands facing the Atlantic and North Sea from Cape Finisterre to Denmark. It resulted in a population so limited down to the eighth century that it could not affect forest, swamp, or maritime resources in any significant way and thus left this part of Europe with a natural environment almost as unexploited or underdeveloped as that which greeted Europeans when they arrived in the Americas during the sixteenth century.

Until the end of the eighth century, the same steady population decline, coupled with German barbarian invasions, Vandal piracy, encroachment by North African bedouins, and the collapse of Roman government, adversely affected Atlantic shores between Cape St. Vincent and Agadir Bay in Morocco and in the entire Mediterranean west of Sicily, with the exception of a brief sixth-century interlude. This turmoil caused considerable agricultural decline and urban decay, especially along North African coasts and between the Ebro and the Tiber, similar to that taking place in Atlantic Europe and producing a world characterized by the same underutilization of available natural resources. This was to continue in both the Atlantic areas and the western Mediterranean, until the situation began to improve during the late eighth and ninth centuries. Until this time, however, we find a prevailing pattern of underdevelopment more significant than in any period since the Greeks, Carthaginians, and Romans had begun to dominate this part of the civilized world centuries before.

We must emphasize, though, that there was a sharp contrast between these maritime areas, where population was scanty and resources came to be underutilized, and the maritime regions to the east of Sicily. Here, with the exception of the Adriatic and the Aegean-Black Sea areas, which will be considered separately, there is evidence that no considerable changes took place until in the seventh century when Persian and Arab invasions modified the pattern of life in Syria, Palestine, and Egypt. Until that time, development along maritime shores continued relatively undisturbed and followed the same general rhythm that had characterized these areas for centuries past.

With this as a general background, let us begin with the first of the newly developing maritime areas to concern us, a most precocious region indeed, and one which suddenly appeared between the Aegean and Black Seas and was centered in Constantinople and the Sea of Marmora. Backward and relatively underdeveloped in Hellenistic times and during the early Roman Empire, this region began to assume a new importance when Constantine picked the small city of Byzantium as his new capital early in the fourth century. Thereafter, the city grew spectacularly and vitally affected the entire Black Sea and Aegean areas nearby. As Constantinople became a metropolis—with a population of between 300,000 and 500,000 by the reign of Justinian—it became closely tied to regional marine ecological conditions, especially timber. The timber resources of this part of the world were considerable, not only those found along the northern Aegean and around the Sea of Marmora but especially along Black Sea coasts near the Bosphorus. Here prevailing winds from the north dumped moisture along the south shores of the Euxine on a scale so great that they caused luxuriant pine and hardwood forests to grow. These provided a constantly renewable and almost inexhaustible supply of timber which could easily be floated south through the Bosphorus to the city located on the Golden Horn and the Sea of Marmora. Here it not only furnished the wood used in the construction of the city itself but also provided imperial and private dockyards of the area with an abundance of timber for shipbuilding.

It is these timber resources which help to explain how Constantinople arose so quickly and how ships were found so easily to provision it with supplies drawn from nearby maritime areas. They also explain why it was here that a revolution in ship construction began—a better, frame-first method very different from that used in classical times—as underwater archeology along Anatolian Aegean shores has revealed. It seems equally probable that this abundance of timber helped cause a second maritime revolution: the shift from heavy pottery *amphorae* to light wooden barrels as containers for transporting liquid cargoes by sea.

If timber was the most important maritime resource in this region, abundant salt was the second, being produced in salt pans in the Aegean world to the south, where ample sunlight made salt production, so necessary to the life of this area, cheap and efficient.[1] We know less about fish as a commodity except that Black Sea fishing grounds provided abundant supplies which could be easily transported to Constantinople via the Bosphorus, whose current flowed south into the Sea of Marmora. When we ask if any ecological changes occurred in this latter body of water due to the rise of a new metropolis on the Golden Horn, it is interesting to note that in Justinian's time whales suddenly appeared here and caused quite a stir—probably attracted by the abundant new supplies of plankton that the city's wastes caused to multiply in the warm shallow waters of the Propontis.[2]

Once established as a vital maritime area by the middle of the sixth century, Constantinople continued to flourish even though during Heraclian and Isaurian times nearby regions in the interior of Anatolia and the Balkans suffered from urban decline and severe losses of population. Constantinople and its environs, however, continued during the next few centuries to utilize the same abundant Black Sea timber and fish and salt from the south. Although after the Fourth Crusade the city suffered a considerable decline in its population, it is interesting to note how quickly it recovered after its conquest by the Ottomans, who at once took advantage of the same timber resources to build warships and commercial vessels in its dockyards, used fish from the Black Sea and Propontis to nourish a growing population, and imported salt from the Aegean to add savor to their diet and to use as a much-needed preservative.

Like Constantinople and its environs, our second maritime region, the upper Adriatic, also began to develop a new importance during the late Empire when the western imperial capital was moved first to Milan, and then to Ravenna. Here, around the shores of the upper Adriatic, were to be found many of the same resources that made Byzantium such an attractive site from a maritime point of view. There were abundant stands of timber along the Dalmatian coast, salt which could be cheaply and easily produced in lagoons near the entrance to the Po, and considerable supplies of fish, thanks to the nutrients the Po and other nearby rivers carried into the Adriatic. There were even two excellent routes into the interior, one leading up-river to Milan and Alpine passes which gave access to France, Switzerland, and the Tyrol, the other leading to central Europe by way of Aquilea, the terminus city for the amber trade from the Baltic.

That this region had become an important maritime center by the fifth century is shown by the fact that the *Notitia Dignitatum* mentions *two* separate war fleets based at ports in these waters and that timber in considerable amounts was exported to Alexandria at the time of Maurice.[3] Indeed, if there is another area in which both the container revolution and the frame-first method of building ships may have begun between the fifth and seventh centuries, it would be this part of the Mediterranean complex of seas.

Important as Ravenna and Aquilea were as centers of activity during the earlier Middle Ages, it was the rise of Venice following the Byzantine loss of the Exarchate to the Lombards and Carolingians that marks a certain coming of age about the upper Adriatic. By the ninth century, Venice was taking advantage of nearby resources in salt to trade as far inland as Padua in Lombardy, while it used abundant Dalmatian timber to construct commercial vessels, some of which not only sailed to Constantinople but also carried timber to Islamic ports throughout the eastern Mediterranean.

From now on, this city on the lagoons parlayed a traffic in these products as well as in iron from Alpine areas to form a maritime empire in the Near East and became powerful enough to capture its mother city of Constantinople in the course of the Fourth Crusade. During these same years, and later on as well, salt remained one of the bases of its prosperity; to the end of the thirteenth century the city continued to find sufficient timber along Dalmatian shores to build numerous ships for its arsenal and provide exports to areas such as Egypt that were deficient in wood. Later on, though, as ships increased in size, it found it necessary to seek suitable ship timber and masts further afield in the Mediterranean-Black Sea area where it had far-flung commercial interests, just as it now needed to tap distant supplies of fish, grain, and other foodstuffs to feed its growing urban population. Until the late eighteenth century it remained a maritime power solidly based upon local Adriatic resources and yet powerful enough to meet the Ottomans on the sea on almost equal terms.

The third maritime area to appear in southern European waters was on the Atlantic and Mediterranean shores of the Straits of Gibraltar. Though there is evidence that this region had been of some importance from a maritime point of view as early as the sixth century, its real claim to maritime vitality dates from the ninth and tenth centuries when, as we have noted, Venice was also becoming a power on the sea. By this time, although pacification of nomadic tribesmen and their conversion to Islam had made possible much trans-Saharan caravan traffic to the Sudan whose gold flowed north to the Mediterranean, it was upon maritime resources that much of the prosperity of Al-Andalus, Morocco, and western Algeria were now based.

First, there was the matter of timber, which was in such short supply in most of the Islamic world, according to Lombard, and so abundant here. Large supplies of timber existed because the prevailing westerlies which blow in from the Atlantic most of the year carried sufficient moisture to encourage the growth of large stands of timber along the Atlantic shores of Morocco and southern Iberia, as they did within the Mediterranean area as far east as Murcia and central Algeria where high mountains close to the sea caught this same moisture. From Valencia to Alcacer do Sol and from Salé to Bougie, then, there existed considerable supplies of timber for building war fleets and commercial vessels. This timber was a critical factor in the effective sea power of the Fatimids and Ommayads during the ninth and tenth centuries and the maritime empires maintained by the Almoravids and Almohads in the Maghreb and Al-Andalus later on, until Christian reconquest of most of the Iberian peninsula had been achieved by the Aragonese, the Castilians, and the Portuguese in about 1250 A.D.

Until this time, however, it was fish as well as timber which helped to bring prosperity to this part of the Islamic world. Partly, these fish consisted of schools of sardines which annually follow coastal currents and the prevailing westerlies along West African shores to reach waters between Portugal, Andalusia, and Atlantic Morocco. Even more valuable, then and now, was an annual tuna run which moved in the same direction, passed through the Straits, and proceeded eastward along the African coast until it reached Sicily, Malta, and Pantellaria. Known since classical times and attracting large numbers of fishermen and merchants, some in the twelfth century from as far away as Genoa, this tuna run, like the sardines, provided this part of the world with a valuable source of protein and important revenues as well.

As for salt, it was produced in a number of salt pans scattered along the coast from Salé in the Atlantic Morocco and the Portuguese Algarve to the Balearics, useful not only for human consumption but to preserve fish catches. It also seems probable that it was during these centuries that the abundant olive oil of Iberia and the sardine and the tuna married to form the preserved fish which still delights our modern palate, though there is some evidence that this actually had been started somewhat earlier, in Roman times.

When the Christian kingdoms of northern Spain had completed their conquest of Valencia, Murcia, Andalusia, and the Algarve, gained control of the Straits of Gibraltar, and established their hegemony over the Maghreb, as Dufourcq has shown, these resources became theirs. It is no accident that they began almost at once to follow fish runs out into the Atlantic, to take over Madeira and the Canaries, and to press on to settle in the Azores, the Cape Verde Islands, and along the coast of West Africa. Although King Dinis of Portugal and his successors thought it wise during the fourteenth century to plant forests to furnish their small realm with adequate timber for their fleets, there is no evidence that either Aragon or Castile lacked for wood, especially in the new arsenal that the latter established at Seville as soon as this port fell into their hands. Indeed, it is hard to imagine how either the Spanish or the Portuguese could have built the great fleets they used in the sixteenth century to expand their power overseas into great empires if they had not built upon those maritime resources which their Islamic predecessors had already begun to exploit in the Maghreb and Al-Andalus.

The last Mediterranean maritime area we will examine appeared quite late along the shores from the Ebro to the Tiber. While this region had attracted Syrian merchants and ships in some numbers in Merovingian times and had seen a brief flurry of local activity on the sea during the early ninth century centered in Pisa and Roussillon, we have to wait until the early eleventh century for evidence of a genuine maritime awakening. At about this time along the Ligurian and Tuscan coasts, the mariners of Genoa and Pisa began to exploit abundant supplies of local timber, take to the sea, wrest Sardinia and Corsica from Moslem pirate fleets, and help the Normans take Sicily. They then went on to raid the great port of Medhia in Tunisia and join other Latins in winning Syria and Palestine from the Moslems during the Crusades.

Genoa and Pisa exploited timber resources along nearby shores which had not been used since early Roman times and were therefore extensive. By the early twelfth century they were also procuring considerable amounts of salt produced in the Narbonnaise and in the shallow *étangs* of the Rhone delta, while they used the Rhone valley itself as a route leading from the important fair of Saint Gilles to the even more important fairs of Champagne and northern France. As for fish, although the mariners made use of local supplies, especially those caught off Marseille and the mouths of the Rhone and Arno as we have noted, by the mid-twelfth century their merchants were bringing tuna back from the coasts of Morocco.

Gradually, however, these cities began to meet competition in their domination of this area's commerce from new centers in the Midi, such as Montpelier, Narbonne, and Marseille, which by the late twelfth century had begun to develop merchant fleets of their own, using local timber and trade with distant areas of the Mediterranean. By the first decades of the thirteenth century these latter were joined by Barcelona, whose Catalan merchants helped Jaime the Conqueror add Valencia and the Balearics to his realms. Later on they joined his successors in dominating the commerce of the Maghreb and Sicily and in establishing commercial contact with the eastern Mediterranean, using Iberian timber resources and salt from Minorca and Sardinia. By the first half of the next century, these Catalans were rivaling the Venetians and Genoese as masters of the Mediterranean and venturing with them out into the Atlantic as far as Britain, the Netherlands, and the west coast of Africa.

It seems clear that until the mid-fourteenth century western Mediterranean timber supplies were sufficient to provide these Italians, Provençals, and Aragonese with all the wood they needed to build their ships and export woods to timber-deficient Moslem shores. For instance, using local supplies Genoa built a great thirteenth-century fleet which transported Louis IX's forces to Egypt at the time of the Fifth Crusade. Aragonese monarchs made use of similar resources to construct the flotillas they employed in Balearic, Valencian, and Sicilian campaigns; and Philip the Fair did the same when he began to form a Mediterranean navy at Aigues Mortes.

By the late fourteenth and fifteenth centuries, however, when northern ship types came to be used in the Mediterranean and merchant vessels increased in size, it seems probable that such timber supplies were no longer adequate. By this time, though, the considerable extent of Genoese and Catalan connections with ports from the Atlantic to the Crimea and Cyprus meant they had transcended any dependence on local timber resources. For instance, now Genoese shipwrights were building galleys in Rouen, Lisbon, and Seville as well as in Pera and Kaffa, just as they were able to tap distant maritime regions for fish, salt, and other foodstuffs. They were even well on their way to becoming partners with the Castilians in the exploitation of the wider world of the sixteenth century.

Turning our attention now to northern Europe, we find our first evidence of a respectable maritime area here dating from the seventh and eighth centuries, when we hear of English and Frisian shipping operating along the shores of the English Channel and North Sea. Soon some of the latter began to sail as far north as Hedeby in Denmark and Birka in Sweden in search of gain. Both they and their Anglo-Saxon neighbors used local timber supplies to build their cogs, keels and other craft, but we do not know whether or not they had yet begun to exploit the herring of the North Sea in a systematic way or where they were procuring the salt they used. At least they had developed sufficient maritime expertise to build a fleet to protect these shores against the Vikings during the reign of Charlemagne and a little later at the time of Alfred the Great to construct the first English navy in these same waters for use against the Danes. Not until the tenth and eleventh centuries, though, do we find any considerable use made of English forests to procure wood to build warships in Channel and North Sea ports for the fleets of the Anglo-Saxon successors of Alfred and for Canute, some of which were vessels of great size. Soon thereafter similar shipbuilding activities were undertaken along continental shores from the Seine to the Elbe under the impetus of William the Conqueror's conquest of England and Robert the Frisian's distant expeditions at sea.[4]

The real growth in importance of this maritime area, however, began in the late twelfth and thirteenth centuries, by which time both the English and the Netherlanders were building fleets capable of trading with the west coast of France for wine and with distant Lisbon, as well as transporting crusading armies through the Straits of Gibraltar and into the Mediterranean as far as the Syrian coast.[5] They also began to exploit the herring fisheries of the North Sea by sailing to the Dogger Banks and developed a lucrative traffic with Norway and Denmark. By now they were also shipping liquid cargoes, such as wine, and fish, grain, and flour as well, exclusively in barrels instead of in pottery containers. In England, at least, the wood they used in building ships or fashioning wooden barrels came from forests protected by a set of unique Forest Laws which kept timber from being wasted by those who used this expendable resource.[6] As for salt, we know that most of it, in England at least, was produced by a boiling process using the same abundant wood employed in the smoking of herring and haddock to preserve them. From the great wine port of Bordeaux to Bergen and

Copenhagen, the cogs, hulks, keels, and barges of this area were plying the seas and earning handsome profits for their English and Low Country owners and shippers.

While the Channel-North Sea area was slowly developing maritime muscle from the ninth century on, the two areas of Scandinavia that concern us—the coast around Bergen and the Kattegat-Skagerrak region—were displaying a sudden burst of sea activity known as the "Age of the Vikings." During the late eighth and ninth centuries Norwegians and Danes began to build oceanic warships and *knorrs*, sail out into the Atlantic and North Sea and raid along the coasts of Britain, Ireland, and continental Europe. The Swedes did the same in the eastern Baltic. By the 870s Scandinavian colonists had begun to settle in Iceland and a century later were established in Greenland.[7]

There is no evidence from this Viking period of the ninth, tenth, and eleventh centuries that either the cod of the Lofoten Islands or those found off Iceland were exploited on more than a local scale, but it is clear that Norway's west coast had become a major shipbuilding area and that Bergen was now the chief port used by those who wished to sail directly west to Iceland and Greenland.[8] Similarly, we have no record of any large-scale utilization of the herring which spawned off Shäne, although by this time the waters of the Kattegat and Skagerrak had begun to replace the Eider-Schlee route across Jutland as the main route linking the North Sea and Baltic, perhaps because now ships were much larger, especially the huge *drekkars* of Scandinavian monarchs, many of which were built in these same waters.

By the twelfth and thirteenth centuries, however, all this had changed. Lofoten cod now helped make Bergen an international port visited by large numbers of English and German vessels. The herring fisheries off Scania had helped to create an international fair which attracted not only nearby German merchants but English and Netherlander traders as well. Soon Lubeckers came to dominate this fair and its fisheries, not only because of their proximity to it but also because they controlled salt exported from Luneville in Saxony needed to preserve the herring for export. Since both the city of Lubeck and much of northern Germany were subject to Danish monarchs down to the 1230s, however, and these same rulers were cooperating with north German noblemen and townsmen in expanding their rule into distant Livonia, there was still little friction between Scandinavians and Germans at the fairs of Scania and elsewhere in Scandinavia. This was to develop later on.

The abundant timber found throughout this entire area made shipbuilding easy, and we know that large warships and merchant vessels continued to be built in Norway down to the end of the reign of Harold Haakonson. The same is true of Denmark during the reigns of the Waldermars, who were able to construct large fleets capable of carrying armies to Estonia during these same years. Perhaps both areas were already exporting ship timber, barrels, and naval stores to the Netherlands and Britain during the thirteenth century. It is clear, then, that by this time two new maritime complexes had arisen in this part of the northern seas, where timber, salt, and fish were playing a major role.

But by the early fourteenth century a number of changes had taken place in this part of Europe, the most important being the almost exclusive domination of these waters by north German merchants and shipping, especially those from Lubeck, Hamburg, and Bremen who had helped organize the German Hanseatic League. Using cogs and hulks which seem to have been better built and to have had more cargo capacity than the vessels of their Scandinavian neighbors and taking advantage of their control of the export of grain and salt to northern ports, the Hansa managed to establish a monopoly over the export of cod from Bergen, herring from Scania, and furs, timber, and naval stores from the entire Baltic. They excluded not only the English and Netherlanders from the North Sea and the Channel from the Kattegat and Skagerrak, but Danes, Norwegians, and Swedes as well. From their factories in Novgorod, Riga, and Bergen to Bruges and the Steelyard of London, the Hansa controlled the trade of the North.

This Hanseatic domination of northern sea-lanes, however, did not last beyond the mid-fifteenth century for a number of reasons. First of all, the Hansa began to face a more effective political opposition from Scandinavians who, having formed a political union at Kalmar, ended Hanseatic control of the vital Kattegat-Skagerrak waterway into the Baltic. At the same time, English monarchs, such as Edward IV and Henry VII, built new fleets and applied new navigation acts to Hanseatic trade with Britain.

Equally important is the fact that English fishermen who were excluded from Norwegian cod fisheries began to catch this fish in large numbers off Iceland, a practice which coincided with important changes in the herring fisheries of the North Sea. By the fifteenth century we have evidence that herring catches off Dogger Bank had increased spectacularly, so much so that most historians have claimed that an actual change in herring spawning took place with Baltic herring changing their spawning grounds to the North Sea. This seems highly unlikely, however. Rather, it seems that London and Netherland urban centers had increased so greatly in population that they poured a larger and larger volume of wastes into the North Sea. These wastes caused an explosion in the North Sea plankton population, which in turn caused the herring to multiply spectacularly. The greatly improved North Sea herring catches of this century, then, were the direct result of a change in the ecology of these waters caused by the growth of London and other nearby cities. This increase made it possible for the English and the Netherlanders of this region to break the Hansa's herring monopoly, just as Icelandic cod played a similar role as regards this variety of fish.

In the third place, these years saw important changes in northern ship types to the detriment of Hansa shipping when early in the fifteenth century a new kind of vessel appeared on both sides of the North Sea. This was the carrick which, though related to both the hulk and the cog, was an oceanic vessel superior to both, representing a mingling of northern and Mediterranean maritime traditions. Like the Portuguese caravels which appeared at about the same time, these carricks gave French, English, and Netherland seamen an advantage over their German rivals who remained faithful to their older models. At the same time in the Netherlands we even find a new type of fishing vessel called the *buss* which made their fishing practices more efficient also.[9]

Finally, this same period saw Atlantic mariners begin to exploit a new and cheaper salt which was produced along the west coast of France by evaporation instead of by mining or boiling. This cheap Borneuf salt and that of Portugal gave an advantage to those Atlantic seamen and fishermen who were closer to this supply than were those who belonged to the Hansa.

By 1500, then, the Channel-North Sea area had again become the leader in northern maritime circles once Hansa domination had come to an end. Although Britain like the Netherlands was by now in part dependent upon the importation of some Baltic timber and naval stores—a dependence which had begun as early as 1350—the fish and salt they needed were now close at hand, and they and the Spanish and Portuguese from near the Straits of Gibraltar possessed superior ships. Thus they could take a lead in the expansion of Europe overseas, where newly found and seemingly unlimited timber, fish, and salt from the wider world, added to their own supplies, were to help them win mastery over the seven seas.

CHAPTER SIX

Ecological Crisis in Fourteenth Century Europe

by Charles R. Bowlus

In the mid-fourteenth century Europeans experienced an event that in our day would be the equivalent of a nuclear holocaust. One out of four persons perished within a span of three years, and the total dead may have surpassed twice the number killed in Europe during World War II. Of course, a nuclear holocaust did not cause this death and suffering for the immediate cause was the coming of the Black Death, a plague bacillus to which Europeans had no natural immunity. Historians are still trying to assess the impact of the plague on European society and institutions during the late Middle Ages and early Renaissance, and the scholarly debates continue. At this point it is clear, however, that the Black Death was not an isolated disaster; no mysterious microorganism in itself precipitated far-reaching social, economic, and political changes, for the plague was but one, albeit a serious one, of a series of crises that shook the foundations of European civilization laid during the high Middle Ages. Some contemporaries thought that the Black Death represented the visitation of God's wrath upon Latin Christendom, punishing men for their sins. Although no modern historian would subscribe to this theory of divine causation, interpreting the Black Death as a kind of *deus ex bacteria,* many believe that the crises of the fourteenth century were caused at least partially by the sins that Europeans had committed against their natural environment during the twelfth and thirteenth centuries; they insist that an ecological crisis was the root cause of the disasters that plagued Europe during the 1300s. R. S. Lopez has argued, for instance, that mortality rates were high, because the lower class population was chronically undernourished at that time and that this was so because the food producing potential of the land had declined due to the ravishing of the environment by Europeans during the two preceding centuries. M. M. Postan, a British authority, has seen the fourteenth century as a classic example of Malthusian economics at work. Population pressed against resources, and no technological breakthrough occurred which might have permitted better resource utilization; thus, famines, riots, and wars became more frequent as human beings struggled for larger slices of a diminishing economic pie until nature struck in the form of plague reducing human population and restoring equilibrium. In Postan's words, "the crises of the fourteenth century were caused by the inordinate expansion of the preceding epoch."[1]

To understand what historians like Lopez and Postan are saying, it is necessary to erase some misconceptions which many well educated persons unfamiliar with recent historical research have concerning the Middle Ages and the Renaissance. The educated generally believe that the Middle Ages constituted a period of economic stagnation that witnessed no social progress, while the Renaissance, which dawned in Italy in the fourteenth century, ushered in a rebirth of the European economy and opened up avenues of social advancement for the talented. Historians also believed these generalizations at one time, but historical research during the past fifty years has altered the picture considerably. Though no historian would deny that the fourteenth and fifteenth centuries were a great period in the history of European art, today the prevailing view is that the fourteenth century experienced a depression that was followed by a slow, halting recovery in the fifteenth. Indeed, Professor Lopez, in a ground-breaking article, "Hard Times and the Investment in Culture," has implied that the artistic achievements of the Italian Renaissance were made possible because surplus capital, which in an earlier period would have been reinvested in commerce, agriculture, and industry, was during the fourteenth and fifteenth centuries invested in the arts due to the uncertainties of the marketplace.

If many historians now believe that the early Renaissance was an age of economic depression, they are convinced that the twelfth and thirteenth centuries were ones of rapid, if uncontrolled and uneven, economic expansion. Even those who regard the conclusions of Lopez and Postan as extreme do not deny that the twelfth and thirteenth centuries were a period of unprecedented growth, and they are hard pressed to prove that the fourteenth century did not witness a slowdown. The debate today centers on the extent of the growth during the earlier period and the extent of the slowdown during the later.[2]

I shall concentrate on the data that is accepted by most historians as accurate and on arguments that have won a large measure of acceptance within the historical community. The story I shall tell is one of an economy that overexpanded relative to existing resources and available technology in the twelfth and thirteenth centuries. My conclusion is that environmental factors, while perhaps not the sole cause of the crises that struck Europe in the fourteenth century, were certainly important contributing factors.

In the year 1050, Europe was a sylvan sea with only isolated islands of human habitation. Although the populations around the hamlets could be quite dense, the forests were seen as the enemy of man, the abode of hobgoblins and demons, unsuitable for human habitation. In contrast, by 1300 there were villages almost everywhere and forests almost nowhere. In 1050 enlightened landowners had encouraged their dependent peasants to reclaim lands from forest, fen, and moor; by 1300 those who were enlightened did everything in their power to prevent the exploitation of what remained of the woodlands of medieval Europe. Granted some landowners, addicted to the joys of the chase, acted out of selfish interests, hoping to preserve their choice hunting grounds, but even their actions demonstrate that there was a growing shortage of game and, thus, that great ecological changes had taken place since 1050.

The great clearings of the Middle Ages began harmlessly. They started on the edges of densely packed villages where potentially fertile but undeveloped lands existed. By the end of the thirteenth century, however, they had spread into the bad lands of Europe, the Black Forest, the Welsh highlands, and into the upper reaches of the Alps. An Alsatian friar, for instance, presents a nostalgic description of his homeland as it had become near the end of his long life around 1300. This land in his boyhood had been sparsely settled, a few scattered hamlets surrounded by grain-producing lands toward the Rhine and a few vineyards along the foothills of the Vosges; near the end of his life all of this had changed. Where there had been villages, there were now walled towns; where there had been forests and swamps, there were villages and grainlands. Viniculture had been extended up the hillsides and large flocks of sheep grazed at higher elevations. Across the Rhine in the Black Forest the process of land reclamation had proceeded even earlier. The dukes of Zährlingen had created a territory for themselves out of a vast wilderness. By 1300 there is evidence from a chronicle set down in nearby Basel that all of this clearing had affected the ecology of the upper Rhine negatively, for the source reports that grain crops were frequently destroyed in the fertile river bottoms due to excessive flooding caused by the run-off from denuded slopes. Moreover, there are reports that pests frequently destroyed crops, that is, the enemies of cereals probably increased along with the area under cultivation. Even viniculture suffered at the end of the thirteenth century, for grapes rotted for lack of oaken casks to store and ship the wine. By the end of the thirteenth century the price of wine was determined by the availability of casks rather than quantity or quality of the vintage.

The great clearings of the twelfth and thirteenth centuries were necessitated by spectacular population increases. Experts in medieval demography agree that the population of Europe as a whole doubled and perhaps tripled during this era. In some regions the increases were even greater. Historians used to believe that population growth was caused by the introduction of a new system of agriculture based upon the heavy, wheeled, mould-board plow, the increasing use of horse power, and a three-field system of crop rotation. No doubt this system increased per capita productivity, freeing peasant labor to clear away forests, build dikes, and drain swamps. This system made possible for the first time the cultivation of much of the low-lying soils of the northern European plain; these soils were heavy and loamy, unexploitable by ancient methods. Yet the diffusion of this new system of agriculture was uneven, and it reached many parts of Europe only after there were unmistakable signs of population growth. Furthermore, this system did not become common in those parts of Europe that witnessed the greatest increases in population during this epoch, for the most noticeable demographic growth occurred in Italy where the new agricultural system was not—indeed *could* not—be introduced, except in the Po Valley. In Tuscany, for example, where records are exceptionally abundant, we know that the population was greater in 1300 than in 1850. Yet Tuscany with its light soils, hills, and vineyards was simply unsuited for this new system of agriculture. The reasons behind demographic growth during these centuries thus remain mysterious. Perhaps growth occurred because of factors beyond human control. Between 800 and 1250 there probably was a gradual warming of the climate of Europe, and many historians are currently studying paleoclimatology in an effort to determine to what extent natural forces caused demographic change.

Be that as it may, the new agricultural system did increase the per capita productivity of the northern European peasantry, thus making it possible to sustain population growth for at least two centuries. Many of the new lands brought into cultivation were virgin, and they were generally very fertile. As a result, many regions produced substantial surpluses during the twelfth and thirteenth centuries. There were vast areas of Europe where there was an abundance of land and a shortage of labor. This land-labor relationship worked to the advantage of the peasantry, particularly in eastern Europe where the landscape was especially suited to this new agricultural system. Landlords in eastern Europe sent agents (*locatores*) whose task it was to encourage peasants to leave the older settled regions of Europe and to settle in the east where they were promised lands and even capital equipment for low rents and few forced labor services. The migration of peasants from the older regions of western Europe into newly opened territories in the east has been compared with the migration in the opposite direction of American farmers from the coastal plains of the Atlantic into the fertile regions of the upper midwest. In the twelfth and thirteenth centuries the word was for some peasants, "Go east, young man, go east!"

Of course, the majority of the population did not go east, just as the population center of gravity in this country only slowly moved westward generations after the first settlers had staked their claims. In the Middle Ages the task of land reclamation could be carried out in the older regions as well as on the frontiers of Latin Christendom. In the heartland of Europe new villages were founded by the thousands during the twelfth and thirteenth centuries. Many landowners lightened labor services and lowered rents and other obligations in an effort to encourage peasants to bring more land under the plow. Although landlords at this time did not understand modern economic theory, their actions demonstrate that they were aware that they could increase their incomes by adopting policies that fostered growth. In the year 1000 A.D. few peasants ran away from their villages no matter how burdensome their lives had become. There was simply nowhere to go; the woods were forbidding and could not sustain large human populations, and in the back of the potential runaway's mind there were no doubt thoughts concerning what would happen to him were he seized by cutthroats and sold into slavery or returned to his master who would surely make an example of him. By 1200 the runaway had many opportunities. He could go east to the Baltic or flee to a free village where a neighboring lord, short of labor, would not return him to his former hamlet. Finally, the peasant could escape to the towns, which were growing in size and number at this time.

There is no better evidence of the growing population at this time than the well documented story of the urbanization of Europe. In the late eleventh century the largest towns in the Latin West had populations of around 10,000 at most, and there were very few urban centers that had that many. In 1300 some of the larger Italian towns had populations that surpassed the 100,000 mark, while some northern ones had from 40-60,000 inhabitants. There were literally thousands of towns of between 5,000 and 10,000 souls, often in places where no urban settlements had existed before. Around the year 1050, towns were several days from one another even for men traveling on horseback; in 1300, settlements recognized as towns were commonly within a day's walk of one another, and new village communities lined the roads between the urban settlements. One of the reasons why peasants chose to stay in the older regions was because there they were within the proximity of rapidly growing urban configurations where there was a demand for their agricultural surpluses and a need for unskilled labor. We know enough about the vital statistics of the medieval town that we can assert with confidence that towns simply would not have grown at the rates they did had there not been substantial immigration from the countryside. Urban careers took time to establish, and, consequently, urban males married late. Urban families were much smaller than rural ones. Therefore, the sustained growth of medieval towns must have been accompanied by even greater rates of growth in the rural areas. The development of urban markets made it worthwhile for the peasant to invest the labor necessary to bring new lands into cultivation. To accomplish these tasks peasants welcomed the birth of sons, and additional clearings could provide lands for some heirs while others sought the bubble fortune in the towns.

By 1300 some of the larger towns of Europe could no longer sustain themselves from agricultural commodities coming from their immediate agricultural hinterlands, and a few urban centers had to import grain from very distant localities. Florence, for instance, could acquire from Tuscany only enough grain to feed the city for five months of the year. At the same time some regions of northern Europe had become grain importing centers. Even some predominantly rural areas had turned to agricultural specialization and to large scale husbandry, exporting such commodities as wine and wool in order to pay for grain imports from elsewhere. It is true that much of the total value of trade in medieval Europe involved luxuries, pepper, spices, silk, fine woolens, ivories, and so on, but trade in bulky commodities was far more significant than once thought. If large surpluses of grain existed near waterways, they could be shipped cheaply to distant ports where shortages existed or where conscious decisions had been made to concentrate on other products or to use the land in different ways. Europe is a peninsula surrounded by the Black and Mediterranean seas, the Atlantic, the North Sea, and the Baltic. Northern Europe possesses large rivers which can be navigated deep into the interior, while most of the major cities of the south lie near the coasts. In the thirteenth century the waterways were utilized to move low-priced bulky commodities from regions where they were abundant to areas where they were scarce. During this century the newly opened territory of eastern Europe became the granary of Europe, a position that it would retain until the nineteenth century. Northern German and Polish cereals became necessary commodities on the Norwegian market early in the century, and regular shipments of grain went out from the port of Bergen to Iceland and even the tiny Greenland community. By the end of the century Baltic grain was essential for highly urbanized Flanders; it was occasionally bought by some northern French towns when local calamities destroyed crops, and it was even beginning to penetrate the British market, competing successfully with wheat produced in the south of England. It was also shipped to the ports of Bordeaux and Lisbon where it was exchanged for wine, a bulky semi-luxury unavailable in the north. Early in the fourteenth century Baltic grain was entering the Mediterranean on a fairly regular basis. At the end of the thirteenth century eastern European cereals constituted important reserves for much of maritime Europe. In the event of local crop failure, or in the case of the interruption of normal channels of supply, Baltic grain could be purchased and famine avoided. But what would happen if crops should fail in a large number of regions during the same year or over a period of years? Baltic reserves were insufficient and transport facilities inadequate to meet contingencies arising from a prolonged crisis in the food supply over a wide geographical area.

The economy of Europe in the late thirteenth and early fourteenth centuries was surprisingly interdependent involving a great deal of specialization. Baltic lords relished the wine of Alsace, while British magnates consumed those of southern France and Iberia, and the Abbot of St. Gall preferred the vintages of northern Italy to those bitter fruits of southern Germany. Centers for the manufacture of fine cloths sprang up in Flanders, English wool fed the looms of the Flemish industry, while Florentine drapers imported fine raw wool from Spain. Milan drew upon the mineral resources of the eastern Alps to become the hub of the arms industry. Splendid falcons reached Europe from far away Greenland, as did walrus ivory, the material from which most early chessmen were made. Saffron from Spain was in great demand in the north. Even sugar was not an unknown commodity, albeit a very expensive one. Northern Europe furnished other regions with raw timber in addition to grain and such luxuries as furs and amber. The specie that was exchanged in these many transactions came from newly opened silver mines in Bohemia. Men constructed ships, barges, and wagons to haul these goods; they opened new roads and passes; they threw up bridges over what had earlier been impassable rivers and gorges.

Accompanying the growth of population and commerce and the rise of towns and cities was the development of more complex systems of secular and ecclesiastical government, the evolution of commercial contracts and banking, and the emergence of more sophisticated views of man and his relationship with nature. In the late eleventh century rulers were illiterate and the nature of their government was personal. In 1300 rulers were universally literate and their government was institutionally based on such concepts as the *status regni,* the *res publica.* If rulers were literate at the end of the thirteenth century, so were merchants. From the end of the thirteenth century our documentation of medieval life becomes enormous. It was certainly not only a few international merchants who were literate, for more than 40 percent of the population of many cities could read. The medieval church did have usury laws, but these were directed against pawnbrokers and others who gouged the poor; the international merchant-banker found it surprisingly easy to circumvent them. The growth of trade and even the growth of royal government was financed to a large extent upon credit, that is, upon interest-bearing loans from commercial banks, such as the Bardi and Peruzzi, some of which were many times larger than the later Medici bank. Early in the fourteenth century the Bardi had branches from England to central Asia, and it was possible for the merchant to travel from London to Frankish Greece armed only with letters of credit, carrying very little specie on his person.

Beginning in the twelfth century men came to develop new attitudes towards nature. Men no longer considered themselves victims of nature, but rather her master. Nature had a rational order, and if man could understand this rational order, then nature could be made to serve mankind. This intellectual view of the relationship between man and nature conformed with the practical experience of men who were not intellectuals. Peasants who were busily clearing away forests could hardly have looked upon nature as a force over which they had no control. Men of the thirteenth century were also fascinated with inanimate sources of energy. The power of the rivers and streams was being used to drive machines, which evolved rapidly and developed multiple uses. In the lowlands of Europe, where waters move slowly, the power of winds and tidewaters were harnessed for the same purposes. The compass appeared in Europe around 1200, and some thinkers toyed with the idea of using the force of magnetism to power a perpetual motion machine. Others speculated about bringing the power of expanding gases into the service of humanity. In the early fourteenth century gravity had been put to at least one useful purpose: to drive the elaborate clocks perched atop magnificent cathedrals and guild halls.

Perhaps the most remarkable and enduring witness to the creativity of the twelfth and thirteenth centuries is the Gothic cathedral, a monument to the engineering and artistic skills of this age. In the cathedral one can see in stone and stained glass a magnificent symbol of the period. It is no accident that these structures arose largely in the towns, for it was the new wealth created within the town walls that made their construction possible. The twelfth and thirteenth centuries when taken together were an age of optimism and progress. Nature was being conquered and society was becoming richer; government could be burdensome at times, but justice was now more impartial. The infidel Saracen still clung obstinately to his blasphemies, but he had been largely expelled from Spain and the holy sepulchre would surely fall once again into Christian hands in just a matter of time. There were schismatic Greeks and heretics to be sure, but the ecclesiastical authorities would eventually bring them around to right reason; man was constructing monuments in stone and glass that reached almost to paradise itself. God was in his heaven; everything was right with the world.

But all was not right with the world. Shortly after 1300 things went wrong. Two centuries of uncontrolled expansion had been purchased on credit using as collateral Europe's natural resources, which were being rapidly depleted. In the fourteenth century nature foreclosed. The resource base simply was not sufficient to sustain growth given the technology available at that time. In the thirteenth century man had seemed triumphant over nature; in the fourteenth century nature turned the tables, and Europeans experienced a series of crises that undermined not only the economy but the ability of states to govern, the power of the church to provide leadership, and the possibility for theologians to explain the world as a rationally ordered whole.

Central to the crises of the fourteenth century was the steady exhaustion of sylvan resources. Wood was for the medieval economy what petroleum products are for that of the t ventieth. It fueled the forges that produced the plows, horseshoes, swords, and other implements that had been necessary during the period of land reclamation. It heated the fortresses of landed magnates, the urban dwellings of wealthy burghers, and simple peasant huts. And, of course, many of the dwellings themselves were constructed primarily of wood. Wood was the basic building material for ships, barges, and wagons. As I have already pointed out, the expanding wine industry annually increased its demand for oaken casks so that wine producing regions suffered acutely from deforestation. And the casks that were shipped from those regions rarely returned. Glass makers consumed thousands of acres of timber while creating such wonders as the Gothic cathedrals. According to modern estimates, it required one hundred square meters of timber to produce one square meter of stained glass. New lands were won for agriculture at the expense of forests, and it was these lands that made possible the surpluses upon which the expansion of the twelfth and thirteenth centuries rested. By the year 1300 more than two centuries of steady expansion of the agrarian economy had led Europeans to base their institutions and their cultural patterns upon the premise that the resources that had enabled this expansion were virtually unlimited. In the year 1050 the forests must have seemed limitless, and there was tremendous waste in the subsequent clearing that took place. In regions where timbers could not easily be floated to market they were simply burned away. In 1300 there were timber shortages almost everywhere, especially in the mining districts where charcoal was desperately needed for the reduction of ores.

The most spectacular example of ecological disaster in the fourteenth century is evidence of general and recurring famine. There had been famines in the twelfth and thirteenth centuries, but those had largely occurred in regions where local crops had failed and cereals could not be imported from elsewhere because of lack of port facilities or financial strength in the region affected. There are no recorded examples of general famines in Europe between 1100 and 1300. In the fourteenth century general famine became common, however, the most serious coming between the years 1315 and 1317. The summer of 1314 had been an unusually wet year, and yields were low all over Europe. When abnormal rainfall continued in 1315, crisis loomed on the horizon. By the spring of 1316 stored reserves had been exhausted and mass starvation stalked the land. In those parts of Europe from which we possess good statistical data, it is known that the price of grain increased from three to five times. Moreover, the data suggests that after 1300 general famine became a specter that Europeans had to face once each decade. In some Flemish towns, which had long been dependent upon imported grain, one person in ten died during the years 1315-17. There were frequent grain riots in the towns and even some reports of cannibalism.

These famines may not have occurred had not the climate worsened in Europe during the fourteenth century. The warming trend that had characterized the preceding epoch ended, ushering in an era of cooler, damper weather. Nevertheless, there is considerable evidence that many marginal lands had been brought into cereal production during the age of agricultural expansion and that these lands were losing their fertility before the fourteenth century had dawned. Even some prime grain lands experienced declining yields prior to the end of the thirteenth century. Animal production was also probably pressing against natural limits—though husbandry has not been as carefully studied as agriculture. Pork, for example, had been a common source of animal protein during the early Middle Ages. The sow is a fine reproductive engine, and piglets can be fattened in the forests and slaughtered in the late fall or early winter. Pig production did not keep pace with that of other domestic animals during the high Middle Ages, however, perhaps because of the disappearance of the forest, perhaps because of the increasing demand for wool, parchment, and vellum that encouraged peasants to raise other animals. The use of the horse as a plow animal had disadvantages that were noted by thirteenth century agronomists. Horses consumed enormous quantities of oats, a significant commodity in the peasants' diet, and in certain parts of Europe there were taboos against eating horse flesh. Although animals contributed manures which could restore fertility to fields, increasing specialization of agriculture and husbandry meant that large herds grazed in the highlands of Europe, far removed from the grain producing bottom lands, where there were only enough animals to provide the peasantry with some high-grade protein and with plow teams. The sources give a clear impression that there never was enough manure available where it was most needed. Moreover, overgrazing in the highlands produced severe ecological damage. For example, in the Alpine districts of central Switzerland, which were rapidly colonized during the thirteenth century, communities reached agreements with one another after 1300 to prevent further clearing and overgrazing because of the danger of avalanches which descended without warning into deep, narrow valleys. All in all, the evidence points to the conclusion that the agricultural economy of Europe approached certain natural limits as the thirteenth century turned into the fourteenth. In spite of an optimistic belief in progress, that man could master nature, no technological breakthrough came forth before a series of crises had taken a terrible toll.

The crisis in the material culture of Europe during the fourteenth century did not cause other crises that afflicted Latin Christendom after 1300. Yet it may have contributed to them. The Babylonian captivity of the papacy, for example, would have occurred with or without an ecological crisis, but the Avignon popes were unloved, and not just because they had changed their residence. The popes of this period were generally able men who actually improved papal administration during their stay on the banks of the Rhone. Indeed, one of the reasons why the Avignon popes were unloved is because they were much more efficient at collecting papal dues than their Roman predecessors had been. What was the reason for the increased efficiency? In a period of economic crisis, when growth was coming to an end, popes had to be more efficient in collecting and husbanding their resources, that is why!

Competition between states became more intense during the fourteenth century. The Hundred Years' War between France and England was only the most prominent of a large number of conflicts that broke out. Commercial centers, such as Venice, Genoa, and Barcelona, were at each other's throats as markets dwindled and international trade became more uncertain. Wars forced rulers to increase taxes at a time when their subjects could least afford it, and they borrowed heavily at a time when they were in no position to repay their debts. In 1341 the king of England abrogated his debts to the Bardi and Peruzzi banks. When the word spread there was a run on these institutions, and the credit structure of medieval Europe collapsed like a house of cards.

There was a striking increase in the number of witch trials in Europe during the fourteenth century. Professor Richard Kieckhefer has studied these and has shown that some were directly related to environmental problems. Crop failures motivated desperate people to accuse their neighbors of engaging in diabolical acts which they thought had precipitated disasters. As the uninterrupted progress of the twelfth and thirteenth centuries came to an end, common people and intellectual inquisitors looked for scapegoats, individuals who had betrayed society by conspiring with witches and demons. Kieckhefer's picture of the intellectual inquisitor reveals a pathetic individual behind the inquisitorial mask. Trained in Aristotelean philosophy, he had been taught that there was a certain order in the world that could be understood by human intelligence. But all of the pieces of this natural order no longer fit together, so he believed that diabolical forces had conspired with human agents to disrupt this natural order of things. In the hands of the inquisitor, harmless superstitions were transformed into charges of diabolism.

In this climate of crisis, it is no wonder that many individuals experienced self-doubt. God was obviously punishing man for his sins. Man must purge the flesh of its sinful nature. Flagellants became a common sight. The Black Death, when it came, was thus only one of a series of disasters, and it reinforced among some of the survivors these feelings of doubt. But if some joined the flagellants, others, such as the witty young men and gracious ladies in Boccaccio's *Decameron,* ate, drank, and made merry. Death, a necessary end that will come when it will come, may seem an unwelcome guest to those upon whom he calls today, but he can be the benefactor to those who can put off his visit until tomorrow. In the mid-fourteenth century survivors mourned their loved ones, and then they rushed to the bank to collect their inheritances. Although uncontrolled population growth had probably been halted prior to the arrival of the plague, this contagion did bring an end to the specter of overpopulation that haunted Europe in the fourteenth century. Moreover, since bubonic plague became endemic, periodic outbreaks acted as a check on population growth for centuries thereafter.

At present it is impossible to assess the full impact of the Black Death upon medieval Europe. Current research, however, has made it clear that some survivors fared better because of the plague than they would have otherwise. Younger sons, who normally could have expected only a paltry share of the family patrimony, suddenly found themselves in control of great wealth as pestilence cut down parents and elder brothers. Some peasants who farmed marginal lands on a subsistence basis found new opportunities when plague struck down farmers in more favorable locations. Workers who survived the onslaught found their labor dearer than it had been before. Does this mean that the Black Death was a blessing in disguise, a panacea that cured the disease of overpopulation? Probably not, because Europe did not recover from the crises of the fourteenth century until the latter half of the fifteenth.

The disasters of the fourteenth century became deeply etched upon the European consciousness, and this in itself may have been one of the most positive results of these crises. The forests did indeed return to much of Europe, and future exploitation was more disciplined, less wanton. Commerce and banking became better organized, though on a much smaller scale. The exploitation of mineral resources became more careful and systematic under the Fuggers in the fifteenth century than it had been under laissez-faire policies of the thirteenth century that had allowed a host of entrepreneurs to devastate mining districts in fierce competition with one another. Also, in the fifteenth century, as Professor Herlihy shows in the next chapter in this volume, Europeans came to look at nature as a source of pleasure and recreation. Nature need not become once again the enemy of man, but it did not exist simply for man to exploit either. Certainly no documents give better testimony to this changing attitude towards nature than do the paintings of fifteenth-century Italy. Finally, the crises of the fourteenth century convinced some that philosophy based upon the writings of Aristotle did not answer all of the problems of man and his relationship with nature, the cosmos, and God. The intellectual movement we call humanism was closely associated with a re-examination of the foundations of Western culture. So there were positive responses to the environmental crisis of the fourteenth century, but the question remains, "unlaid like a ghost," is it possible for a society experiencing long-term economic growth to come to terms with the limits of that growth before crisis makes that society painfully aware of those limits?

CHAPTER SEVEN

Attitudes Toward the Environment in Medieval Society

by David J. Herlihy

In the present, anxious examination of ecological issues, what is the value in the exercise we undertake here, a review of those attitudes toward the environment which developed in western Europe across the thousand years of medieval history? Ours is not the first society which has lived, or believed that it was living, under conditions of ecological stress. For ecological tensions are not exclusively the product of modern industrialism. Traditional societies, to be sure, did not possess the powerful and potentially destructive technologies our own civilization now wields.[1] But neither did they possess the powerful, and potentially protective technologies we moderns can also marshal. People of the past were far more subject to, than master of, environmental forces. Their lives, institutions, societies, and values were in consequence highly sensitive to slight changes in ecological balances. In reconstructing the experiences of our predecessors, we can hope to discern ways in which ecological stress, or its absence, has affected societies in the past and may again in the future.

The Middle Ages of European history, extending from the fall of classical antiquity to the opening of the New World, have these two further claims to our interest. The period is long, and the social changes experienced across them many and profound. And medieval people were, for the most part, articulate and have left in their recorded learning and literature an abundance of comment on the world as they saw it and their own reactions to it. There remain, to be sure, enormous gaps in our knowledge of medieval society and its history. Hard data, reflective of the real conditions of life, while not altogether absent, have survived only sporadically. For many places and periods we can view life as contemporaries perceived it, but not as they truly lived it. Still, even these perceptions can be revealing, and we are rarely without some notion of basic demographic and economic trends. Medieval history, it might be claimed, forms a large museum of cultural attitudes toward the environment, which were formed at different times, under different material conditions, and over many centuries. Here, we shall visit that museum. We shall review how medieval people looked upon their surroundings and inquire, as best we can, why they saw things as they did.

It is possible, I believe, to distinguish within medieval culture four attitudes, or sets of attitudes, toward the environment. The first, which we shall call "eschatological," was founded upon an effort to assess the present state of the world, or of nature, in the light of the presumed ultimate destiny of the human race. The second, the "adversarial" in our nomenclature, implied a fear and awe of nature as the abode of mysterious monsters, spirits, and powers inimical to men. There is also discernible in our medieval sources a contrary opinion which we shall call the "collaborative;" it affirmed that man, like nature itself, could shape and change the environment and even aid in the process of cosmic fulfillment. Finally, to some medieval thinkers, particularly those caught in the trammels of an increasingly complex social life, the contemplation of the natural world was a source of psychological and spiritual refreshment and renewal. This fourth attitude toward nature we shall call "recreational."

Each of these attitudes comes into prominence during certain periods of medieval history, and we shall examine them in the order given above. We do not imply by the arrangement of our discussion that one attitude supplanted another at a given moment in time. None of these approaches to the physical environment was ever completely triumphant, and none completely suppressed. They were all of them included in the heritage that the Middle Ages passed on to the modern world; some of them, or elements of them, may even be recognizable today, even by those who knew little about their medieval origins.

In exploring eschatological attitudes toward nature, the period of our initial interest is the centuries of transition between the ancient world and the Middle Ages, primarily from the third through the fifth centuries. During this epoch, the Christian religion, for long an obscure sect born of obscure origins in an obscure corner of the ancient world, unexpectedly arose to claim the assent of emperors to wax triumphant within a sinking empire. At the same time, the intellectual leaders of the new religion—"fathers of the Church" in the traditional terminology—were elaborating fundamental attitudes toward God, man, nature, and the world which long continued to affect the beliefs and behavior of medieval people. It is therefore of obvious importance for our understanding of medieval—and modern—history to inquire what the Christian fathers thought of the physical environment.

The Biblical basis of Christian, or Judeo-Christian attitudes toward nature and the world has recently attracted the comment of both historians and theologians. One of the most provocative of these commentators has been the distinguished historian of technology, Lynn White, Jr.[2] In his view, Judeo-Christianity is the most anthropocentric of all the major religious traditions the world has known. Here, the capital text is God's commission to Adam, recorded in the book of Genesis: "Increase and multiply and fill the earth, and make it yours, take command of the fishes in the sea and all that flies through the air and all the living things that move on the earth."[3]

God, in other words, had placed all of nature under man's dominion, to do with as he pleased. This promoted, in White's assessment, a kind of ecological triumphalism, a sense that in their dealings with the material world, men need only consult their immediate self-interests. They had no moral responsibility for the survival and welfare of the things and creatures which God had created only to serve them.

In the long history of Christian theology, surely many thinkers interpreted these verses from Genesis in the manner White describes. And, yet, historically this view emerged only belatedly. Particularly in the writings of the Christian fathers, there is found no celebration of man's dominion over nature. The fathers are much more concerned with the wages of original sin and with the plight of postlapsarian man. Here, the critical text is also from Genesis—the curse which God laid upon the earth as a direct consequence of Adam's sin:

And unto Adam he said, Because thou hast hearkened unto the voice of thy wife, and hast eaten of the tree, of which I commanded thee, saying, Thou shalt not eat of it: cursed is the ground for thy sake; in toil shalt thou eat of it all the days of thy life; thorns also and thistles shall it bring forth to thee; and thou shalt eat of the herb of the field. In the sweat of thy face shalt thou eat bread, till thou return unto the ground.[4]

By God's curse, earth was rebellious to man, its appointed master, just as man had been to God. In the phrase of the greatest of the fathers, St. Augustine, nature had been "vitiated" by Adam's sin, thus the presence of natural evils in the world: famines, disease, death, and the other miseries of our earthly sojourn. "The accursed earth," writes St. Augustine, "shall bring forth thorns and thistles for thee. Are you not ordained for sorrow and not for delights?"[5]

Moreover, in their common opinion, the Christian fathers maintained that the human population had already reached its maximum size, that the earth was saturated with people, and that all its resources were claimed or exhausted. Ecological pessimism, not triumphalism, infuses their writings.

Tertullian, for example, the first Christian to write extensively in Latin, describes the crowded world of about A.D. 200:

Everything has been visited, everything known, everything exploited. Now pleasant estates obliterate the famous wilderness areas of the past. Plowed fields have suppressed the forests; domesticated animals have dispersed wild life. Beaches are plowed, mountains smoothed and swamps cleaned. There are as many cities as, in former years, there were dwellings. Islands do not frighten, nor cliffs deter. Everywhere there are buildings, everywhere people, everywhere communities, everywhere life.[6]

Tertullian does not rejoice in the human conquests he describes. Rather, in phrases which anticipate the warnings of the English clergyman, Thomas Malthus, he lists the penalties of overpopulation:

Proof [of this crowding] is the density of human beings. We weigh upon the world; its resources hardly suffice to support us. As our needs grow larger, so do our protests, that already nature does not sustain us. In truth, plague, famine, wars and earthquakes must be regarded as a blessing to civilization, since they prune away the luxuriant growth of the human race.[7]

Ecological pessimism is evident, too, in a related patristic belief in the advancing senility of nature and the world. In the middle third century, St. Cyprian, who, like Tertullian, was a North African, vividly describes the world's movement toward an early end, a movement which man himself, its supposed master, can neither stop nor slow:

You ought to be aware [he writes] that the age is now senile. . . . There is a diminution in the winter rains that give nourishment to the seeds in the earth, and in the summer heats that ripen the harvests. The springs have less freshness and the autumns less fecundity. The mountains, disembowelled and worn out, yield a lower output of marble; the mines, exhausted, furnish a smaller stock of the precious metals: the veins are impoverished, and they shrink daily. There is a decrease and deficiency of farmers in the fields, of sailors on the sea, of soldiers in the barracks, of honesty in the market place, of justice in court, of concord in friendship, of skill in technique, of strictness in morals. When a thing is growing old, do you suppose that it can still retain, unimpaired, the exuberance of its fresh and lusty youth.[8]

St. Augustine, who died in 430, the most prolific and influential of the Latin fathers, faithfully repeats both these themes. The world is saturated with people, there is no more space to fill; nature has grown old, and human history is approaching its term.[9]

With these assumptions, the fathers faced an evident problem in interpreting the Biblical injunction: "Increase and multiply, and fill the earth." The command, in their exegesis, had indeed been applicable to Adam and Eve and to their immediate descendants—a single couple or a small group of persons set within an empty earth. But now the command had been changed, indeed abrogated, by what Augustine calls "the mystery of time." As the world was already crowded with people, "no duty of human society" (the phrase is again Augustine's) required marriage and further procreation.[10] "There is not the need of procreation," he writes, "that there once was." "The coming of Christ," he elsewhere alleges, "is not served by the begetting of children."[11] Even within the Christian community, marriage was a concession grudgingly conceded to the morally weak; in Augustine's words, "marriage is not expedient except for those who do not have self-control."[12]

The Christian fathers do not disguise their aversion to sex, marriage, and procreation. Even within marriage, intercourse could never be without fault, since in performing it passion dominated reason; all persons on earth were consequently conceived in iniquity. But would not the growth of the Christian community increase the number of saints in heaven? No, reply the fathers, for the number of saints had been fixed from eternity and could not be altered by human behavior. "The number of saints," says Augustine, "will be perfect, none fewer, and none more."[13] In a widely shared view, the saints would exactly replace in their numbers the fallen angels.

In lauding virginity over marriage, and childlessness over parenthood, the fathers had to face the evident protest that if all men and women followed their advice the human race would not last a generation. This would be, Augustine responds, entirely a good thing. It would indicate that the number of saints had attained its predestined size, and the City of God perfectly populated. The Christian fathers refused to concede that there was any social or religious value in the propagation of the human race or in sheer numbers of people.

How are we to explain these extraordinary patristic attitudes, that the human race now filled the earth to saturation, that the bounty of nature was declining, and that the further propagation of mankind served no purpose? Are these prejudices no more than an odd display of perverse asceticism? In fact, these patristic attitudes repeat the judgments of numerous pagan writers, whose personal values were far from ascetic. One of the most eloquent descriptions of the world's senility comes from the Roman poet and Epicurean philosopher Lucretius, in his poetic essay "On the Nature of Things."

Furthermore [he affirms] of her own accord [earth] first created the shining grain and smiling vineyards for mankind. She herself produced sweet fruits and fertile pastures, which now can scarce grow anything, for all our toil. And we exhaust our oxen and our farmers' strength, we wear out plow-shares in the fields that barely feed us, so much do they begrudge their fruits and increase our labor. And now the aged plowman shakes his head and sighs again and again, to see his labors come to naught, and he compares the present age to days gone by . . . and groans to think of the good old days, when . . . life was easily supported on smaller farms. . . . The gloomy grower of the old and withered vines sadly curses the times he lives in, and wearies heaven, not realizing that all is gradually decaying, nearing the end, worn out by the long span of years.[14]

Then, too, some pagan authors show as much opposition to marriage and to procreation as do the Christian fathers. An early monument of this hostility is the so-called *Liber aureolus,* or "Little Book of Gold," written by an Athenian philosopher and student of Aristotle named Theophrastus. The original text has not survived, but the theme so appealed to the Christian father St. Jerome that he copied large sections of it into one of his own efforts to disparage matrimony.[15]

The behavior of pagans in the classical world also indicates a reluctance to marry and to multiply. The Greek historian Polybius, who died in 122 B.C., observed that the inhabitants of the Greek cities no longer cared to marry, or if they did marry they reared only one or two children in order to keep inheritances undivided. In the first century after Christ, the Latin poet Ovid says of Roman ladies: "Rare is the woman who in this age wishes to become a mother."[16]

How are we to explain this widely diffused opinion, shared by both pagans and Christians, that the world was both burdened with people and worn out and that there was no particular value in the further propagation of the human race beyond its present numbers? The paradox is that many modern historians believe that the Roman empire was eventually undermined by an opposite factor, by insufficient rather than excessive population, by a *penuria hominum*, or shortage of men. But this was not the common perception of contemporaries, and the world in history, as the world today, is as people perceive it. The ancients rather show an acute consciousness of limits. They could discern no unclaimed space, no new frontiers, no fresh worlds to conquer. Their technologies held out no hopes of brilliant, new departures. The prospects for humanity appeared singularly dismal. At best, the generations of the future might live exactly as their forebears. At worst—and this was the more likely outcome—they would fall back from the present enjoyment of a totally realized world and exist within an aging, deteriorating social and material milieu. There were grounds for ecological pessimism.

It is interesting to observe how the people of the ancient world behaved in the conviction that the farthest limits of human expansion had been reached. Among pagans, the presumed density of human settlement justified both the avoidance of marriage and the practice of effective means for limiting children within it. The many who did not marry were, in the common pagan ethos, free to indulge themselves in all varieties of non-reproductive sex, including homosexuality and pederasty. The Christian fathers in particular have given us lurid depictions of pagan sexual mores, which have earned for late antiquity its durable reputation for unbridled sensuality. They doubtlessly exaggerate, but the picture they paint is not completely false. Within marriage, the most effective method of limiting children was infanticide. Except among the Jews and, later, the Christians, infanticide did not excite the ancients' moral indignation.

In the developing Christian culture, the low value given procreation is implicit in the high praise of virginity commonplace in Christian writings. The varied responses to perceived ecological stress in late antiquity are thus singularly paradoxical. On the one hand, among some social segments the belief that the world was filled seems to have promoted the acceptance of nonreproductive sexual practices and the toleration of infanticide. On the other hand, the same sense that the earth was saturated with humanity helped instill among parts of society an extreme asceticism and repression of all forms of sexual activity. Pagan sensuality and Christian asceticism may appear to us distant viewers as diametrically opposed values, but in fact they generated the same demographic consequence: a stable, even declining, population.

One final observation may be made concerning the Christian fathers' ecological attitudes. The patristic assumption that the further multiplication of the human race did not increase the number of saints or advance the cause of Christianity persists through the subsequent centuries of Western history. Ultimately, this belief that the sheer size of population had no religious or social value may have facilitated the adoption in Western societies of alternate forms of population control, of practices that fell somewhere between the total rejection of sex advocated by the Christian fathers and the practice of infanticide common among most ancient peoples.

We now turn to the view of nature as our adversary. The world of the early Middle Ages, from the sixth through the tenth centuries, differed markedly from its classical predecessor. The ancient cities, the cultural and social centers of antique Mediterranean civilization, lost size and vitality. Trade and monetary exchanges withered, and agriculture became the principal, nearly exclusive support of the people. From what we can surmise of ecological conditions in the early medieval centuries, the population remained extremely small, but it seems not to have been distributed evenly across the countryside. Rather, the inhabitants of Europe seem to have been clustered in numerous small but packed communities, "population islands," as historians now call them. During the reign of Charlemagne, for example, in the early ninth century, when suitable documentation aids our vision, we can observe the surprising situation of overcrowded communities set in the midst of an extensive, largely empty wilderness.

Why did these medieval settlers not depart from the crowded villages and seek new living space in the forests and wastelands that hemmed them on every side. Historians now commonly speak of the force of "internal constraints" which long blocked such an outflow of peasants from the old centers of settlement. These constraints included the strong ties of kinship, the need for protection in a still disturbed and dangerous world, and serfdom, or the discipline required on the large estate or manor. Important, too, in turning the growth of these communities inward rather than outward seems to have been a psychological factor, a deeply seated fear of the wilderness, a sense that harrassed mankind could not readily cope with the mysterious beings and forces that made their abode in forests and deserts.

The religious traditions of Judeo-Christianity reinforced this fear of the wilderness. In the Old Testament, the wilderness is sometimes presented as the opposite of Paradise; unlike the garden of the blessed, it is the home of demons and death.[17] Christ himself was tempted in the desert. From the second century after Christ, hermits such as St. Anthony fled to the desert and there engaged in epic struggles with demons. Their victories over the devils won them fame as athletes of God but left undisturbed the close association of wilderness and evil. Still, while Christianity may have contributed to this suspicion of the wilds, this attitude of fear seems to have been founded upon continuing popular and pagan traditions which viewed the forest as enchanted or sacred, worthy sometimes of worship and always of awe. St. Martin of Braga in Spain, writing in the sixth century, complains of peasants, superficially Christian, who continued to burn candles before rocks and plants, by rivers and at crossroads, who offered sacrifices of fruit and wine to trees and honored streams by placing bread upon their waters.[18]

Among the cultural monuments of the early Middle Ages, the one that perhaps best illustrates this awe of the wilds is the Anglo-Saxon epic poem, *Beowulf,* written by an unknown author probably in the tenth century. The poem manifests a basic tension between human society and the surrounding wilderness—fen, moor, and sea, and the terrible beings they harbor. The symbol of human society is the mead hall, where warriors gather with their chief to drink in fellowship. The *Beowulf* poet takes no delight in the works of nature but only in the works of men: their halls, armor, cups, and rings of burnished gold. The mead hall and its treasures are the antithesis of the somber world of nature.

At the beginning of the poem, Hrothgar, king of the Danes, had constructed the largest mead hall ever built, called Herot. But in so doing he has impinged upon the domain of darkness, and the monsters that defend it are quick to repulse this human incursion. Grendel, a monster of obscure, uncertain form, attacks the hall at night and repeatedly carries off human victims. The Danes can do nothing, and Herot remains deserted for twelve years. The monster and its wilderness have apparently prevailed. But then, word of the affair reaches the distant land of the Geats, and Hrothgar's plight evokes the sympathy of the hero Beowulf. With his band of warriors, he comes from across the sea to aid the king. In violent struggles, he kills first Grendel and then his angered mother, who emerges from the depths of the sea to avenge her son's defeat. In the third part of the poem, Beowulf is forced to fight yet another ravaging monster, a dragon which inhabits cliffs overlooking the sea.

In spite of these successes, a pessimistic fatalism pervades the poem. Beowulf is a doomed hero and king, and even his people the Geats are apparently destined to disappear. The battles against the horrible beings of the night must be fought, but ultimately the best of men will perish in the struggle. The poet laments:

> Who knows when princes
> And their soldiers, the bravest and strongest of men,
> Are destined to die, their time ended,
> Their homes, their halls, empty and still?[19]

Frequently in the literature of the subsequent medieval centuries the forest is presented as the antithesis of civilized human life. One poignant illustration of this comes from the twelfth-century *Romance of Tristan and Iseult*. Tristan enters into an adulterous love affair with the wife of his uncle, King Marc of Cornwall, and the lovers are found out. Violators of the fundamental laws of human society, they can find a home together only in the wilderness. Pursued by their enemies, they flee into the forest. There, each looks upon the other and meditates upon the costs of their adulterous affair. Tristan, Iseult says in her heart, might now be foremost among knights, winning wealth, honor, and fame among men; instead, he lives in savagery. Iseult, Tristan reflects, might be reigning in splendor as an honored queen, in palaces hung with silks; now she lives amid brambles. Love has cost them both the comforts and honors of civilized life. The wilderness which alone welcomes them is the negation of ordered human society and the punishment for those who would violate its rules.

The people of the early Middle Ages, in sum, nurtured fearful attitudes toward their natural surroundings and expected hostility in return. Can this be surprising? These small human communities were fighting for survival. Low technological skills gave them little confidence that they might ultimately prevail and no assurance that the wilderness might not in the end reclaim their fields and their mead halls. Perhaps this attitude is typical of poor and rural societies, which struggle to win sustenance and support from a grudging earth.

From about the year 1000, European society embarked upon a

period of sustained growth which continued until the early four-teenth century. Through changes too complex to rehearse here, the internal constraints that had kept the population packed within the settlement islands now loosened, and Europeans poured forth from their former homes. In part, they moved into the surrounding forests and wastelands and, through extensive clearances, enlarged the cultivated areas of Europe and multiplied its supplies of food. In part, too, they penetrated beyond Europe's former frontiers: east-ward beyond the Elbe River, along the south shores of the Baltic Sea and the course of the Danube; southward through the Iberian peninsula; and even across the waters of the Mediterranean Sea into Palestine, through armed pilgrimages known as crusades. Trade simultaneously revived, and towns, for the first time since the fall of classical civilization, acquired vitality. Within towns, markets and industries took root. Medieval society, once a simple association of peasants, priests, and warriors, now became increasingly differ-entiated. The new social system required merchants, accountants, artisans, clerks, administrators, lawyers, and numerous other specialized and skilled individuals.

The dependence of society upon special skills helped promote a reform in educational institutions of which the chief monument was doubtlessly the new universities. In the opinion of most historians, these profound social developments also depended upon the emergence of a new collective psychology and a new view of man and of nature. The artisans and professional persons had to be self-conscious, aware of the world around them, of the goals they wished to achieve, and of their tools and materials available to them. They also needed confidence in their own training and abilities. Unlike the tremulous peasants and warriors of early medieval so-ciety, they were sure that they could both understand and utilize the natural forces at work in the world.

Within this larger, more diversified, and richer society, there further occurred a renaissance of formal intellectual analysis and, indeed, of extensive cosmological speculations. Over the past dec-ades, many scholars have been actively reconstructing the new cosmology, particularly as it was elaborated in schools of northern France, from the twelfth century. These thinkers—William of Conches, Bernard Sylvester, and Alan of Lille, among others—were strongly influenced by the ancient philosophers, notably Plato, but their thought still reflects the interests and aspirations of twelfth-century society. A principal concern of this new cosmology was an analysis of the creation and development of the world. They were in particular interested in the relative contribution to cosmological formation of three operators: God, nature, and man.

Gilbert of La Porrée, for example, poses the disingenuous question: To what extent can cheese, or shoes, or other artifacts of the human economy, be regarded as the creations of God? In responding, Gilbert affirms that God, the first principle, made the universe, in the sense that he created *ex nihilo* its basic elements. In this regard he can also be regarded as the maker of cheese and shoes. But, Gilbert further notes, many objects in the world are the products of recent generation. All plants and animals fall into this category; they are born and they are subject to eventual decay. God did not and does not create directly the living things we see around us. The force that assures the continuing generation of like from like is nature, and it includes in its domain all things corruptible and renewable. But even nature cannot be considered the immediate creator of cheese and shoes. There is a third maker at work in the world, and this is man. He uses the materials provided by God and replenished by nature, but he adds his own creative imprint to what he does.

The high place accorded nature in the replenishment of the universe implies further that the natural order is autonomous and self-sustaining, not subject to God's arbitrary interventions. Miracles can, of course, occur, but they represent a suspension of the natural order, not its normal operation.

Other thinkers of the twelfth century go beyond Gilbert in the praise they bestow on nature. Drawing inspiration from Plato's *Timaeus* and the ancient commentaries upon it, they argue that nature serves not only the function of forming like from like but also decorates the universe. Much in the manner of Plato's demiurge, it brings the elements of original creation into a true order or cosmos. Nature could indeed be regarded as the *anima mundi,* the soul of the world, which lends form to the universe and assures the harmonious balance of all its parts. In an impassioned poem, Alan of Lille addresses nature with an almost religious fervor:

> Child of God and mother of the universe
> ....
> Peace, love, virtue, governance, power,
> Order, law, end, way, leader, source,
> Life, light, splendor, beauty, form,
>   The rule of the world.[20]

But man is creator, too, who imitates both God and nature in his actions. In making his cheese and his shoes, man recognizes his own needs. William of Conches presents this striking analysis of the operations of an artisan:

The work of an artisan is a work that man engages in because of a need, as making clothes for protection against cold or a house against bad weather. But in all that he does, the artisan imitates nature, for when he makes clothes he fashions them after the natural disposition of the body's members; and when he makes a house he remembers that water that collects on flat surfaces makes wood rot, whereas it flows down off slopes and cleanses them, so he makes his house peaked.[21]

The universe, in sum, was the work of artisans working in tandem: God, to whom we owe the original elements; nature, which forms and renews the cosmos; and man, who is conscious of his own needs but who makes, in conformity with nature, cheese, shoes, and the other products of his economy.

Unlike the Christian fathers, the men of the twelfth century did not gaze forth upon a senile world in which all space had been claimed and all resources utilized. It is worth noting, too, that, unlike the Christian fathers, the thinkers of this period often encouraged marriage and procreation and give no indication that they believed the world already to be filled. In Alan of Lille's allegorical poem, the *Complaint of Nature,* Nature herself in allegorical representation urges men and women to use their natural hammers and anvils in the multiplication of their kind.[22] The thirteenth-century French poem, the *Romance of the Rose,* similarly exhorts the reader to maximum reproduction: "Plow, for God's sake, my barons, plow, and restore your lineages."[23]

The sense of limits, in other words, which pervades the writings of the Christian fathers, here has faded. In this collaborative attitude toward the environment we at last encounter a kind of ecological triumphalism, a belief that man the maker can shape the world according to his needs and multiply his own numbers with impunity. The root of this new approach to the material world seems not to be in citations from Genesis but in the experiences of a young and growing society. Amid expanding frontiers, new towns, new trades, and professions, the limits to growth may well have appeared distant indeed.

This ecological optimism and collaborative attitude toward nature doubtlessly sustained the growth of medieval society until about 1300, but the great expansion of the central medieval centuries came at a cost. Even before 1300, the population of western Europe seems to have attained extraordinary dimensions. The province of Tuscany in Italy, for example, where our records are particularly good, reached by circa 1300 the probable figure of two million persons. Not until after 1850 was that region of Europe again to contain a comparable population.[24] The swollen size of medieval communities has convinced many historians that the Black Death of 1348, and numerous other plagues, famines, and wars of the fourteenth century were not fortuitous acts of God but manifestations of a fundamentally Malthusian crisis.[25] The troubles of the closing Middle Ages seem to have undermined the self-confidence of the earlier period and to have favored, in some segments of medieval society, a return to the patristic belief that the world had grown old and that the end of time was approaching.[26] The supreme confidence and optimism of the twelfth century did not entirely dispel older views of man and his relation with the world.

One other novel set of attitudes toward the environment gains prominence in medieval culture from the twelfth century. This is the contemplation and use of nature for recreational purposes. In this cultural posture, the natural world, real or imagined, promises psychological or spiritual renewal, a release from the tensions and melancholy of everyday life.

This attitude makes its appearance in close association with new groups in medieval society: university students, the "wandering scholars" of the twelfth century; knights and nobles, who were gathering in the princely courts of Europe; and the townsmen, who were also elaborating their own cultural values. The paradox, of course, is that the recreational use of nature first appears among those social groups that live most distant from it, in towns and courts, amid artificial surroundings.

Among the "wandering scholars" of the twelfth century there takes root a tradition of Latin poetry called "goliardic." One of the commonplace themes within that tradition is the beauty of spring, the call to love and joy it inspires. To cite only one of countless goliardic celebrations of idyllic nature:

> The beautiful face of the earth
> Smells of green grass
> The pine puts on its leaves
> The painted tribe of birds sing
> The meadows bloom, the recreation of the young.[27]

There is an irony here, in that the poet apparently does not know that the pine is evergreen; nonetheless his mood is unmistakable.

Tributes to the beauties of spring are no less common in the tradition of troubadour, or courtly poetry, which first appears in the courts of southern France in the twelfth century and soon thereafter is imitated in all the European languages. Peire Vidal, a troubadour of the twelfth century, thus affirms that the lover of nature will be rewarded with joy:

> Great joy have I to greet the season bright,
> And joy to greet the blessed summer days,
> And joy when birds do carol songs of praise,
> And joy to mark the woods with flowerets dight.[28]

Across the continent of Europe in the late Middle Ages, poets in their varied accents invite their listeners to visit with them idyllic woods and meadows bathed in spring or guide them to entirely visionary realms, to the earth in its golden age, or to Arcadia, the fabled homeland of carefree shepherds. Paeans to real or imagined nature arise from unexpected quarters. The Florentine Lorenzo de' Medici, for example, who ruled his native city for more than two decades in the fifteenth century (he died in 1492), was the scion of a long line of bankers and a banker himself. For all his bourgeois interests, in one of his stately poems he dwells lyrically on the course of a mountain stream, the Ambra, which tumbles down from the Apennines. Among his major literary efforts is a poem entitled the *Selve d'Amore,* the "Woods of Love"; in it, he expatiates on the power of love not only to ennoble the lover but also to transform the world around him and restore the Golden Age of endless spring.[29]

Are these poetic expressions no more than empty literary conventions, untouched by authentic aspirations? The love of rustic surroundings seems to have run deeper than that. In 1336, for example, in what is sometimes viewed as the first conscious act of tourism, the Italian humanist Francesco Petrarch climbed Mont Ventoux, the highest mountain in Provence. His reasons for the venture are revealing: troubles had buffeted his life since early childhood, and the mountain offered a sense of stability and eternity. At its summit—with the aid of St. Augustine's *Confessions,* to be sure—Petrarch turned his mind to lofty contemplation on the wonders of creation and man's place within it.[30]

About 1400, a Florentine merchant named Giovanni Morelli urged the readers of his memoirs to avoid melancholy at all cost. One effective way of dispelling depression was to ride "for solace" through the countryside, in the freshness of the morning or during the evening hours.[31] In his *Four Books on the Family,* written in the 1430s, the prominent humanist Leon Battista Alberti urges his readers to spend as much time as possible on their country estates, not only to benefit from its clean water and pure air but to take advantage of its spiritual satisfactions. "What person could there be," he asks, "who could not draw pleasure from the villa?" Life in the countryside, claims Alberti, renders him who is old young again, vigorous, clean and good. Nature, he seems to argue, is restoration.[32]

A sense of the recreational powers of nature is even more eloquently expressed in religious currents of the Middle Ages, particularly those inspired by the "little poor man" of Assisi, St. Francis, who died in 1226. The son of a merchant who rejected the life of getting and spending demanded by the new commercial economy, Francis, at least as legend describes him, gave individuality and dignity to the animate and inanimate beings and to the forces that filled and moved the natural world. In his celebrated *Canticle to the Sun,* he lavishes thanks and praise on brother sun, sister moon, and the stars; brother wind, and air and clouds; sister water; brother fire; earth, which is both sister and mother; and sister death.[33] The familial terms he uses implies that all creatures are siblings and all should serve one another. He thus instructs the wolf which was terrorizing the people of Gubbio to mend its ways; the wolf obeys and lives its days in peace with sheep and men.[34] In his sermon to the birds, Francis congratulates them on their beautiful plumage and comfortable life and urges them to show their gratitude to God through singing. Men, too, should number their blessings and in gratitude abandon strife and war. His message seems to be that if all beings in the universe recognized God's good providence over them they would respond with joy and live in peace one with the other. There is no suggestion here of ecological imperialism. One day, Francis is said even to have freed some caged doves, as all creatures in the universe should enjoy liberty. The universe was, or should be, composed of a chorus of creatures, brothers and sisters every one, living together, singing together, in harmonious praise of their maker.

The economy of the new medieval cities took their inhabitants from the close contact with nature characteristic of rural life. But the urban milieu seems also to have sowed among the townsmen a sense of alienation from, or discord with, the cosmic order. The result was the growth of these extraordinary cults of the natural, manifest in both the secular and religious values of the epoch. These attitudes also entered into the heritage the Middle Ages bequeathed to the modern world.

Over its long duration, in response to the changing social and demographic conditions it faced, the medieval world thus developed and explored a wide range of views concerning the environment. The Christian fathers were convinced that the world was filled with people and its resources exhausted. They saw no need for further procreation, but no future either, different from the present for the human race. The only hope was eschatological—the final consummation of the earth. The harrassed communities of the early Middle Ages rather conceived themselves as locked in an uneven struggle with a hostile nature which they could battle, but never truly overcome, in spurts of heroism. The truly aggressive ethic toward the environment, which has remained for better or worse part of Western culture, seems to have been the product of the eleventh and twelfth centuries, an age of vigorous expansion on almost every level. But the parallel development of a sentimental attitude toward nature implies that this image of man as creator of the world after nature and God did not satisfy the psychological needs of all medieval people.

These ecological tensions and cultural responses thus marked the course of medieval history. In our own efforts to develop an adequate response to our own ecological tensions, we should not neglect the experience, perhaps even the wisdom, accumulated during these thousand years of Western history.

PART FOUR

THE ECOLOGY OF THE MODERN WESTERN WORLD

Introduction

by Charles R. Bowlus

That science and technology can define and solve almost all human problems has become an axiom of modern industrial societies. Though there be dissenters among us, this faith is so deeply rooted among the current heirs of the Western tradition that, in spite of warning clouds on the horizon, few of us can envisage a convergence of circumstances that might result in such a total breakdown of environmental systems that science and technology might be powerless to deal with the situation. If there exists in modern industrial societies a general faith in the efficacy of science and technology, there is little agreement among us as to what exactly constitutes valid scientific knowledge and how that knowledge should be applied. Nor is there an awareness among members of the educated public that science cannot offer us absolute truth about the nature of the universe but can only give us hypotheses which partially explain observable data and which are inevitably super-seded by new hypotheses which likewise are only partial explanations. Moreover, scientists approach problems from the standpoint of their individual disciplines, and they use methodologies which, though valid in examining fragments of reality, are totally useless in explaining relationships among different kinds of phenomena that make up the totality of any natural system. As for the application of science, there are bitter disputes concerning which scientific theories should be converted into human technologies and what should be the roles of government and private industry in such conversions.

The last three essays in this volume, written by a geographer, a historian, and an economist, address these questions directly and leave the careful reader with the uneasy conclusions that perhaps our faith in science and technology is unjustified by the historical record, that perhaps applied science is often pseudo-science, that engineers are so far removed from the forefront of science that they necessarily apply obsolete theories, and that simplistic theories, which offer only momentary solutions to pressing immediate problems, are preferred, even if a more complex and comprehensive body of knowledge is available which might make longer range solutions possible. Finally, these essays give the impression that scientists have remarkably little power to change the institutions and the conventional wisdom of the society of which they are a part.

John Culbertson, whose chapter appears last, goes to the heart of the matter when he shows that much of modern economic theory has been based upon oversimplified assumptions concerning the nature of science. In the seventeenth century the Copernican Revolution culminated in the works of Newton who described planetary motion with seductively simple mathematical formulae which were perceived as an expression of natural law. Enamored by the harmony and simplicity of the Newtonian system, eighteenth-century intellectuals asserted that human societies must also be governed by natural law. In 1776, Adam Smith argued that the law of supply and demand was for the world's economy what the law of gravity was for the solar system. Just as God had formed the matter of the planets and had devised the law of gravity to regulate the revolution of the spheres, so had He created human beings and had invented supply and demand to govern relationships between them. Once God had performed this act of creation and had established the rules of the game (natural law), He did not interfere. As God had left the planets wheeling through space in splendid isolation governed only by His law, so the state should grant each individual maximum freedom to pursue his economic needs governed only by the law of supply and demand. Culbertson argues that this application of Newtonian physics to the realm of human beings was not science but pseudo-science. During the eighteenth century such simple laws were appropriate to explain the motion of large inanimate bodies in the heavens, but even then it was a folly to presume that similar simplistic laws could be applied to human beings, who belong to the complex realm of animate things which science can never completely understand, much less describe with a few simple equations. Adam Smith and his followers dabbled in ideology rather than engaging themselves in disciplined science. They were successful, indeed, but their accomplishments came in the field of rhetoric, not science. The success of Smith's ideology in the United States led Americans to cheat and destroy aboriginal populations and to devastate the environment to a point where now it will be difficult to repair the damage. Culbertson says that only a true science that recognizes the complexities of living organisms and the tentative nature of all scientific knowledge can save us from self-destruction.

In the first essay Thomas Glick makes an appeal for an interdisciplinary analysis of urban ecosystems. As he demonstrates, specialists tend to approach urban problems from the assumptions of their discipline which has resulted in a less comprehensive definition of the urban environment. Because specialists in the scientific community cannot agree, public officials are generally at a loss when it comes to dealing with urban environmental crises, which inevitably arise from an ecosystem that is inherently unstable due to species packing. Thus, responses tend to be limited in nature and correspond only to the interests of elites who wield power in any given society. Professor Glick has a concrete example of this thesis in the "Great Stink," which ascended from the polluted waters of the Thames to spread over London in 1858. Although the problem of the Thames pollution had been troublesome since the Middle Ages and had become even more apparent with the industrial growth of the city during the first half of the nineteenth century, authorities had been forced to deal with the problem in a piecemeal fashion due to the lack of an established body of scientific knowledge and an almost total absence of national policy. The "Great Stink" arose, however, at a time when a comprehensive solution to the problem of Thames pollution was not inconceivable. Science and technology had been fused in England in the eighteenth century to create the world's first industrial society. There was in England a widely held belief in progress through the application of the human intellect. Citizens had already banded together in pressure groups dedicated to forcing the government to come to grips with the problem, and freedom of the press guaranteed public discussion. Not even ministers of parliament from far away districts could ignore the "Great Stink," for the Indian mutiny forced parliament into an unusual summer session while rancid fumes filled the chambers. Yet the "Great Stink" did not result in a comprehensive solution to the problem of Thames pollution. Scientists disagreed, engineers were hopelessly behind the times, and elites chose to ignore the most up-to-date scientific analysis, favoring those solutions in best accord with their immediate aims and interests. Thus, outdated theories prevailed which were sufficient to remedy the stink but incapable of solving the problem.

Just as Professor Glick chronicles a split in England between chemists and engineers on one side and biologists and physicians on the other, Carl Moneyhon shows how divisions among conservationists, preservationists, and ecologists prevented any comprehensive solutions to the environmental problems that arose in the United States as the frontier closed at the end of the nineteenth century. Although there was a general perception of the limits of natural resources in this country at the turn of the century, experts differed so much in their approaches that the movement which aimed at the creation of a national resource policy failed. Once again, the group that offered the most sophisticated analysis of the problems, ecologists, discovered that their ideas were too complex and too revolutionary to find application. Professor Moneyhon's contribution is also linked with Professor Culbertson's insofar as laissez faire attitudes were a major factor in paralyzing governmental institutions headed by Theodore Roosevelt's handpicked experts. Indeed, so strong were attitudes against any federal interference with the "invisible hand" that even the conservationist movement was split into antagonistic camps, those who favored a comprehensive governmental policy and those who were convinced that the private sector could best solve the problem. Fear of the loss of individual economic liberty meant that whatever solutions were eventually achieved were accomplished by large corporations, which resulted, paradoxically, in the disappearance of smaller enterprises and inevitably the loss of economic independence by most Americans.

All in all, the concluding essays of this volume might well leave the thoughtful reader in a melancholy mood, for they question the capacity of the most advanced science and technology to come to grips with the pressing problems of the twentieth century; even more, they demonstrate that much of what we call science is in reality ideology in an academically respectable guise. These chapters raise many fundamental questions which must be addressed if our culture, as we know it, is to survive. Should we start viewing our unbridled faith in the inevitability of scientific and technological progress as a part of the problem instead of its solution? What are the long-range implications of unplanned change? Will attempts to order change lead to undesirable consequences, such as complex and authoritarian governments, or will they lead to equally impersonal multinational corporations responsible to no one and no culture? To restore the balance between man and nature must our culture be destroyed as was that of the Roman Empire in the western Mediterranean? Or must we learn to live with nature under such restrictive governments as that of ancient China or medieval Byzantium? Can we avoid such natural and social disasters as occurred in fourteenth-century Europe? The authors and editor of this book do not have the answers to these questions; however, we do hope we have provided food for thought.

CHAPTER EIGHT

Science, Technology, and the Urban Environment: The Great Stink of 1858

by Thomas F. Glick

Environmental history may be described as that in which the unit of analysis is the ecosystem. It seeks, therefore, to account for systemic changes, over time, in a variety of environmental settings. When dealing with wilderness, forest, or agro-ecosystems, the historian has at his command tools of analysis in the form of modern studies of how these ecosystems work, and these can be easily extrapolated and applied to the past. With regard to urban ecosystems, however, the situation is more problematical, since ecologists have yet to provide any global, or even partial, models to explain them. Lacking an analytical framework, the urban environmental historian explores a virtually uncharted frontier.

Three areas of scientific inquiry likely to yield information about the city as an organic system are ecology, epidemiology, and climatology. Ecologists have generally been disinterested in man-made environments, and those who have dealt with urban phenomena have concentrated upon specific populations (birds and flora, typically) without generating holistic theories of interaction. Since, historically, microbes have been such significant members of urban biotic communities, one would expect to turn to epidemiology for clues to their function in an urban setting, a man-made environment which seems to have been so ideal a microbial habitat. But epidemiologists work with models which, while stressing biotic interactions, only pay lip service to the specific physical and climatological patterning that urban environments introduce into the profile of disease. A related field, medical geography, has been more concerned with the socio-economic, rather than environmental, parameters of disease. In many ways, climatologists have been most concerned with the city as a natural system. Not the least of their accomplishments, they have provided the clearest definition of what, in natural terms, a city is. But on the whole they have been reluctant to deal with the biotic concomitants of urban climate, and the subdiscipline biometeorology has concerned itself almost wholly with human beings, while ignoring the rest of the biotic community.

What is a city to an environmental historian? From an organic perspective, the best answer is provided by climatology. A city is a place characterized by a permanent heat island, differentiated from the ambient countryside both in summer and in winter, not only in terms of temperature but also of humidity and water-storage capacity. Permanent heat islands seem to exist in settlements of urban density with populations of around 12,000, although this minimum may be unrealistic depending on the scale of urban-rural differentiation deemed significant. The main utility of the heat island concept is to provide a measurable boundary to the urban area with detectable systemic ramifications, particularly in the provision of new or expanded niches for certain species of plants and animals.

But if we are to deal effectively with cities as ecosystems we must have at least a tentative model of systemic interaction. In a recent paper, "Urban Ecosystems and Urban Biogeography," Anthony Davis and I suggested that urban ecosystems resemble those of islands. In them, one finds a characteristic reduction of the number of animal species, as the extension of human settlement has resulted in the displacement of many species previously present and the overrepresentation (packing) of a relatively small roster of synanthropic species—animals attracted by man and man-made environments—and the parasites of such animals. Considering vegetation, cities also betray insular characteristics, with large cities resembling small islands (great isolation, fewer species) and small cities resembling large islands (greater species variety by virtue of corridors to the countryside). Although higher plants exist in greater variety than the higher animals, they are subject to the disturbances provoked by the urban environment, and the packing displayed by animal species is in itself a powerful indicator of ecological instability.

There are two primary causes of urban ecological instability. First are the physical structures of the city, which destroy the habitats of many species (while creating a certain number of new habitats, to be sure). Second is the overburdened biomass of the urban area, owing to the density of settlement, the necessity of provisioning the city with organic matter (food), and the inevitable retention of organic waste within the system. For all these reasons, urban ecosystems are lacking in many, if not most, of the homeostatic controls built into natural systems. Urban ecosystems are easily disturbed, and their resilience after perturbation is dependent on sociocultural as much as natural factors. Therefore, the environmental historian views urban history as the attempt by human societies to supply the lacking controls by cultural means, among them the application of technology, scientific knowledge, and institutional arrangements devised for management of the urban environment.

Before the nineteenth century, human efforts at stabilizing an unstable system were limited to a few expedients available to pre-modern technology. The primary strategy was to flush the city through with clean water. This approach was institutionalized in some cities, such as Valencia, where irrigation water was reserved for periodic flushing of the city's sewers. It is possible that in irrigated areas the necessity of having an urban water system allowing for both arterial and venal functions was suggested by parallel systems of irrigation and drainage ditches. In most medieval towns, however, water supply was the main concern, with drainage at best an afterthought. Efforts to deal with the unsavory aspects of species packing remained an ideal rather than an accomplishment. The Pied Piper of Hamlin is an apt symbol.

The complexity of environmental phenomena provides a constant challenge to the historian, suggesting areas of inquiry that include a mix of biotic, physical, and socioeconomic factors. An example of the kind of hypothesis that should concern urban historians is that of W. C. Turner on the historical development of chronic bronchitis in England. The primary lesion in this disease is caused by the spores of molds (species of *Aspergillum* and *Cladosporium*) which excite an allergic reaction in lung tissues. These spores were present in the soil of previously agricultural land on top of which workers' quarters were built in industrializing towns. The overcrowding of urban slums, by raising air humidity, encouraged more active growth of the fungus already present and increased structural dampness by condensation. Moreover, owing to industrial concentration and the location of industry near working class neighborhoods, the residents of such districts were subjected to the aggravating effects of air pollution on the primary lesion. Not all urban environmental problems are medical, but disease-related issues provide an easy pathway into urban ecology because they involve the necessary linkage of a number of species, under identifiable physical conditions (i.e., temperature, humidity).

The case of bronchitis is an example of the use of present-day medical knowledge to generate an historical hypothesis. Another avenue of historical inquiry is the retrieval of observations of vanished urban habitats and the reconstruction of ecological processes now lost. An example is provided by the habits of the sewer rat in nineteenth-century London. The ecology and ethology of *Rattus norvegicus* has been studied recently in a "natural" burrowing habitat specially built for the purpose of observation. *Norvegicus* has not been studied in the sewers. But in the past century, the natural history of the sewer rat was fairly well known, having been described to naturalists by "flushermen" who observed the animals underground. This data has not been used by contemporary students of the rat.

The sewers of pre-metropolitan drainage London were built of rectangular earthenware and brick conduits arched over on top, which formed ledges at inverts where smaller sewers joined larger ones. These ledges were the preferred habitat of the Norway rat, which flushermen encountered there sitting in clusters. This subterranean habitat had a number of distinguishing characteristics. First, the rats only lived and bred in the sewers; they did not feed there, except in those sewers adjoining slaughterhouses or markets. Second, although the Norway rat predominated, the arboreal black rat (*Rattus rattus*) was also seen, a fact only rediscovered in the 1950s. Third, flushermen reported that, contrary to general perceptions of sewer life, the rat was the *only* animal living in the sewers.

From the point of view of sanitation, the most interesting aspect of sewer-rat ecology was not their role as vectors of disease but the mechanical interference the rats introduced into the sewage system. The rat colonies described by flushermen occupied areas of six yards by four yards honeycombed with tunnels. The problem was that the rats destroyed the brickwork of the sewers by burrowing through it, "thus constructing lateral cesspools the contents of which permeate the ground and filter into the wells. In making these excavations moreover they invariably transfer the earth to the main sewers, and form obstructions to the flow."[1] The pipe drains with smooth barrels favored by the sanitarians were bite-proof, but the rats (in the characterization of the same observer of 1850) took revenge in ruining newly-laid sections of pipe "by burrowing under them, and causing them to dip and open at the joints.'' The new pipes forced a habitat shift, but in both cases the rats were able to enhance the spread of water-borne disease by mechanical, rather than biotic, intervention.

The unit of analysis in urban environmental history, in summary, is an ecosystem which is unstable owing to the packing of animal species, whose variety is practically reduced to human beings and their parasites; a narrow roster of synanthropic species (rats, cats, dogs, cliff-dwelling birds, etc.) and their parasites; and a rich animalian lumpenproletariat of insects and microbes about whose natural history we know little. All of these draw their sustenance from an exogenous food supply, vastly increasing the biomass of the city and stimulating further packing. Depending on a variety of factors, the more a city grows, the greater its inability, owing to cost factors, to remove the excess organic material. It is this relationship which is at the heart of the sanitation "crisis" of Victorian London. I use the word "crisis" guardedly: to the extent that they are systemically unstable, cities may be regarded as being in a constantly critical state.[2]

Sewage problems in London can be traced back to late medieval times. London's environment became severely overcharged with refuse in the early 1370s and again in the early 1420s, the clustering of complaints recorded in the municipal Letter Books doubtless reflecting population growth.[3] Underlying this overcharging was an historical process set in motion by the growth of the population and the expansion of the physical structures of the city which had the result of progressively reducing the surface stream water available for refuse removal. As the city grew larger, there was less "natural sewer" capacity in the form of streams to evacuate those latrines which were not built over cesspools, as well as to accomodate other urban waste.

A growing population dumps more stream-blocking waste into its natural watercourses, but at the same time the discharge of those same streams is being reduced by urban growth itself. As more and more buildings are constructed, pavement laid down, or unpaved streets made impermeable by the packing down of their top layers, the total surface that is impervious to water expands, run-off increases, and as a result there is less groundwater contribution to stream discharge. More and more refuse is being dumped into less and less water. Demand for fresh drinking water from sources outside the city is related to this process, partly by the physical diminution of local supplies and partly by the increasing pollution of what remains. Therefore, in spite of the fact that water supply must be planned for and drainage very frequently is not, the two systems are influenced by the same dynamic process.

In such times of severe overcharge of waste, one notes the massing of latrines over surface streams, the inability of the streams to carry the excess burden, and inevitable pollution of the Thames, partly because the streams discharged directly into it, partly because what could no longer be dumped in a stream was carted to the river. Since stream flow diminished over time, pressure mounted to do away with them entirely, giving rise to the phenomenon of London's "buried rivers."[4] The response of public officials was alternately harsh and lenient—lenient when pressures for use fell or because there were no viable alternatives, harsh when conditions became too obnoxious to bear.

To consider the fate of two such streams, the Wall Brook had long been used as an open sewer. In 1313 and again in 1344 citizens who had built latrines over it were required to remove them, to no avail, because in 1383 building latrines over it was declared legal, provided that no additional refuse which might block the water's passage be thrown in. In 1422, a complaint was lodged against the "great nuisance and corruption from the ordure of [a] privy, which comes from London Wall and runs down to the Thames through Wal-brooke."[5] Finally in 1462 all latrines over Wall Brook were abolished and the stream itself vaulted over. According to John Stow, portions were covered over as early as 1300; by 1603, when Stow wrote, the course of the brook was "hidden underground, and thereby hardly known."[6]

The lower course of the Holebourne flows by Flete Prison and was known as Flete Ditch, receiving the waste of the prison and, in 1355, of eleven latrines and three sewers. The result was that the ditch, which in its normal condition should have been ten feet wide and deep enough to float a boat carrying a tun of wine, was completely stopped up. In 1388 there were more complaints about privies, although some were designed to facilitate their cleaning, and the ditch continued to serve as a latrine site, doubtless because it was better endowed with water than others. It reappears in nineteenth-century deliberations over metropolitan drainage as "Flete Sewer."

During the same period, pollution of the Thames was frequently reported. In 1357, the king complained that he had observed "dung and laystalls" along the banks of the river and had "perceived the fumes and other abominable stenches arising therefrom."[7] The clogging of the lanes leading to the river and of the river itself and the use of the river by butchers as a dump for entrails were also noted, as was the lowering of the fish population in the river's water. Probably the fish were less affected by pollution than by the destruction of habitat by dumping along the banks.

The response of town officials to these severe problems was in all cases reactive. Action was taken only when matters became unbearable, and such action was ineffective, as is proven by the constant repetition of the same complaints. There was no technological response beyond the occasional scouring of ditches and the attempt by some latrine owners to void their privies in such a way as to cause the minimum disruption to the stream. Sewage was not subject to any overall plan, lagging in this respect behind street-cleaning which was carried out by "rakers," organized by ward.

The organization of water supply stands in contrast. The city built a reservoir at Tyburn in the mid-thirteenth century and piped water into the city through a conduit. The reservoir was a response to water lost to the city through pollution of the Thames and the diminution of the number of wells. The management of the water supply "became a model for all civil enterprise."[8] It had a specialized bureaucracy of wardens and fiscal officers, the latter managing the revenues assigned specifically for the maintenance of the system. It is this latter aspect that most merits comment. Water-bearing systems, whether for supply or drainage, require secure capitalization and effective management if they are to function efficiently and reliably. Therefore, urban environmental problems have tended to generate bureaucratic machinery to deal with them once a certain threshold of perceived need is passed.

London seems to have had no man-made sewer system until after the fire of 1666. Thereafter the system grew throughout the eighteenth century in steadily increasing increments, reaching a level of exponential growth between 1827 and 1851 which brought the total length of sewers to forty-nine miles.

Medieval Londoners exhibited a limited capacity to deal with sanitary crisis: legislation to prevent or retard waste build-up and the tapping of new water supplies in response to the drying up or pollution of older ones. In Victorian London, if society's organizational and technological capabilities had grown, so too had the magnitude of the problem. Technical and scientific specialization, moreover, had markedly increased the range of responses, which differed according to the social and professional background of the persons involved. Here we examine a number of Victorian approaches to the problem of urban drainage in general and of river pollution in particular, to suggest areas of research for the study of similar problems elsewhere.

Edwin Chadwick, the leader of the Public Health Movement, had been agitating for some twenty years prior to the Great Stink of 1858 for a metropolitan approach to drainage as well as other sanitary problems. He was blocked by two political problems; first, the unwillingness of Parliament to deal effectively with these matters (owing to the unwillingness of non-London members to commit their constituents' tax monies to solving London's problems), and, second, the related issue of the lack of any effective regional authority which could overcome the jurisdictional tangles inherent in the dispersion of power among the various boroughs of the city.

His drive for metropolitan drainage stymied, Chadwick turned to house drainage, promoting the installation of water closets in new houses and the replacement of cesspools by water closets in old ones. Since the water closets ultimately had to drain into the river, Chadwick's plan contributed to overloading the Thames with sewage, bringing about the Great Stink. By the end of 1853, about one-tenth of the homes in London, or 27,000, were drained by pipes.

In developing a general approach to water pollution and the health of the city, Chadwick and eventually Parliament, too, were swayed by the investigations and pronouncements of a number of different scientific and technical groups. Indeed, Chadwick had sought as a matter of policy to involve scientists of different disciplinary backgrounds in the sanitation movement. He had secured the appointment of Richard Owen, the physiologist, and Henry de la Beche, the geologist, to the Sewers Commission in 1848, and when he became chairman of the General Board of Health he appointed as secretary the engineer Henry Austin, brother-in-law of Charles Dickens.

The architect of metropolitan main drainage was Sir Joseph Bazalgette (1819-1891), who served on a variety of commissions, beginning with the Metropolitan Commission of Sewers in 1848. He designed a system of intercepting sewers to discharge the sewage of the city into the river well below the city, but the Board of Works was not given full power to act until August 1858, when the government was at last jolted into action by the Great Stink. Bazalgette and other engineers held that the problem was a mechanical one to be solved by filtration, dilution, and diversion, and that the state of the river water, while disgusting to the senses, was not in itself a danger to public health.

In this, he was supported by British chemists, nearly all of the most prominent of whom participated in the discussions over water in the 1850s and 1860s. In report after report, and in testimony before parliamentary commissions, chemists like Edward Frankland, Augustus William Hofmann, William A. Miller, and William Odling gave the river a clean bill of health, flying in the face of what seemed to medical opinion the obvious evidence of the senses.

Chemical orthodoxy was stated in a 1851 report on the chemical quality of the supply of water to the metropolis by Miller, Hofmann, and Thomas Graham. The chemists' findings stressed the Thames's great capacity for self-purification (a theme consistently stressed by chemists and engineers through the decade), whereby impurities were leached out by filtration through sand and by aeration in the natural course of the river's flow, so that except in extraordinary circumstances drinking water could be obtained "entirely free from suspended solid matter, or mechanical impurities." Moreover, the mineral contents of the water were not injurious to public health, and the hardness of the water acted to inhibit putrefaction. Its disadvantages were that high summer temperatures made the water less palatable and promoted the decomposition of organic material, that it was liable to turbidity from floods ("flood tinge," a yellow color which could be precipitated out by adding one grain of alum per gallon of water), and that it was subject to contamination by town sewage and run-off from manured fields. At present, such contaminants were diluted, aerated, and destroyed by oxidation—the self-purifying power of the river—but, the chemists warned, sewage contamination

cannot fail to become considerable and offensive with the increase of population, and the more efficient and general drainage of towns. And it appears to be only a question of time, when the sense of this violation of the river purity will decide the public mind to the entire abandonment of the Thames as a source of supply, unless indeed artificial means of purification be devised in the meantime and applied.[9]

In other words, the contamination was more aesthetic than lethal and was subject to amelioration through mechanical means.

The reason why chemists could make so blithe an assertion has to do with the prevailing views on the nature of microbial life in the water. The report continues:

The rapid production of animacules in Thames water, when aided by light and warmth, although not in itself a source of danger, evinces the abundant presence of organic matter, which if not rapidly assimilated by these lower orders of animal beings, might render the liquid repulsive, and in all probability actively injurious to the human constitution.[10]

The notion that animacules were harmless was the opinion of Justus Liebig, Hofmann's teacher, who exercised great influence over English chemical opinion. Liebig believed that infusoria were simply a sign of the presence in the water of decaying organic material, which attracted the harmless animacules who fed upon it.

Not all scientists were content with Liebig's opinion, however. In cross-examination by a parliamentary commission the same year, a microbiologist, Arthur Hill Hassall, was asked for his opinion regarding Liebig's assertion that "it is quite certain that water containing living infusoria becomes a source of oxygen gas when exposed to the action of light; it is also certain that as soon as these animals can be detected in the water, the latter ceases to be injurious to plants and animals." Hassall replied that he did not concur in this opinion to any extent. Hassall's rejection of Liebig's views followed a heated exchange during which the biologist attacked the whole notion of the relevance of chemical analysis to public health.

I consider one of the most important contaminations to which water is subject, is that by organic matter: all that chemistry can do in reference to the detection of that is, to designate it under certain decimal figures, or describe it under the head of 'traces;' the microscope will do infinitely more than that; it will tell whether the organic matter in the water be dead, and if dead, whether animal or vegetable; and it will tell us whether it is living, and if living, whether it be animal or vegetable, and also the kind and species.

Not all animal matter could be filtered out by mechanical means. Further, he interpreted the presence of infusorial life in the water in a sense diametrically opposed to that of the chemists. "Their presence is a clear indication of impurity when they are found in the water in any number; and when they are found in large number, the water must be to a considerable extent impure."[11]

Hassall had found large concentrations of infusoria in the Thames in the vicinity of bridges, which is where the main sewers discharged. When asked to account for the fact that Graham, Miller, and Hofmann had found no animacules in their samples, he replied:

I account for that in this way, if the fact can be satisfactorily accounted for at all, that not one of those gentlemen has published any observation on the subject connected with the use of the microscope and consequently it is questionable how far they were qualified to examine the water microscopically.[12]

Between Hassall's opinion and that of the chemists was an unbridgeable gap. Alfred Swaine Taylor, professor of chemistry at Guy's Hospital, testified that animacules were not injurious and that the prevailing opinion was that they improve the water by removing organic material and by setting free oxygen which aerates the water. Swallowing a small number of infusoria, he judged, was not harmful to health. Liebig is a very excellent judge upon these matters, and he considers that those animals are beneficial to the water. If the water were really contaminated by sewage, the infusoria would die.[13]

Health was endangered by polluted water not through the action of infusoria but rather by miasma emitted by decaying organic material. This was the view of chemists generally, and their entire methodology was directed towards the detection of organic material in water. Frankland called such traces "the skeleton of sewage" and, in his opinion, the presence of nitrates and nitrites in river water was a sign that sewage had been discharged into it. This opinion was supported by an influential physician, Henry Letheby, who on the eve of the Great Stink (March 1858) still held to Chadwick's pythogenic theory of contagion. "Experience has shown," he remarked, "that whenever putrefying organic matter comes into contact with soluble sulphates, it decomposes them, or causes the evolution of sulphuretted hydrogen [hydrosulphate of ammonia]." The quantity of sulphates had been shown by chemists to increase in the Thames moving downstream. Sulphuretted hydrogen was the same "miasm" that caused malignant fevers on the African coast, according to Letheby, and was produced in the Thames when the tidal sea water mixed with "fresh water charged with putrefying organic material." This problem could be alleviated by applying lime to the water, which was an imperfect process but the most cost-effective deodorizing technique available.

To one who believed in the miasm theory of disease, deodorization removed the pathogenic substances in the air. In closing, Letheby repeated the chemical maxim that "the Thames possesses the means of self-purification, which is fully equal to the contaminating injury to which it is at present exposed." The sewage itself, by virtue of its passage through the sewers is "so much agitated and broken up . . . as to be in a very advanced stage of putrefaction" so that when it reaches the Thames it begins to oxidate and quickly becomes diluted and harmless.[14]

It will be noted that there was a perfect fit between the findings of the chemists and the plans of the engineers who sought to cure the problem by "mechanical" means—aiding Father Thames in his self-purification by providing the water supply system with sand filters and by adding certain reagents to the water which would precipitate the organic residues out.

Most physicians knew otherwise. Since John Snow had traced the source of cholera to a well in Soho in 1849, a number of statistical-geographical studies had established the coincidence between disease and sewage. The voice of medical opinion, *The Lancet*, repeatedly warned of the impending danger. "Is it too late to raise the voice of alarm?" *Lancet* editorialized in July 1857. "Is it too late to rescue the atmosphere of this metropolis from pollution and its inhabitants from pestilence and death?"[15]

Although the Thames had consistently reeked in summertime for a number of years past, its condition reached the crisis dimension known as the Great Stink in June 1858. Near the end of the month, with the Stink casting a pall over the city, *The Lancet* rejoiced: "Fortunately, the hideous—the truly horrible, state of the river Thames is at last, not only attracting universal attention, but it is exciting a feeling of public indignation which will not be easily repressed. Many years have passed away since we first directed attention to the subject: and when discussing the foul state of the Serpentine, we predicted that the Thames would become in the condition of a common sewer, if the filth which flowed into it from thousands of sources were not directed into some other channel." *The Lancet* believed the river to be a source of disease, although it still held to a miasmatic theory: "It is truly terrible to contemplate what may be the result should a pestilential disease now burst forth, having its origin in a poisonous air produced by the decomposition of enormous masses of organic matter."[16]

On July 10, *The Lancet* admitted that "we regard this stench with philosophic admiration, as being a beneficent natural warning of the putrescent change which is at this moment evolving miasmata, such as might otherwise secretly lay waste our homes with zymotic disease. We have a certain feeling of satisfaction in hearing that the Chancellor of the Exchequer, Mr. Gladstone . . . [has] been forced to beat an ignominious retreat from [the] committee-room, handkerchief to nose. Honourable gentlemen and noble lords would never know how bad it is to wear tight shoes if they did not pinch."[17] The fact that Parliament could not conduct its business (the India Mutiny was underway) without the constant reminder of the river's odor provided the major stimulus to the solution of London's sewage problem.

The Stink produced a flurry of activity amid general uncertainty as to what course really ought to be taken. The windows of committee rooms at Parliament were opened and hung with canvas soaked in chloride of lime to deodorize and purify the air—the idea of Goldsworthy Gurney, a Parliament staffer and self-taught engineer. This was not the first time that Parliament had endured the noxious smells of putrescent sewage. In 1855, Gurney had suggested connecting the sewers under the houses of Parliament to the updraft in the Clock Tower, thus voiding the obnoxious odors. He installed valves at certain points in the sewers to trap the gases, which were drawn by steam-jet to a decomposing apparatus in the tower. In this fashion, according to Gurney, 25,000 cubic feet of effluvia per minute passed through the apparatus and up the tower.

During the Great Stink, Gurney went a step further. Would it not be possible, he reasoned, to run pipes from the sewers of London to direct the sewer-gas into high towers which, when ignited, would rid the city of noxious gas and, at the same time, provide a pleasant, blue nocturnal illumination. He sealed the Victoria Sewer and piped gas through New Palace Yard and up the new clock tower. A match was lit and went out. Sir Joseph Bazalgette then discovered that the pipe leading from Victoria Sewer had been blocked—luckily, it turned out, because the gas in question was a mixture of sulphuretted hydrogen and coal gas, the former emitted by the sewage, the latter by a broken gas main. Had the blockage not occurred, the tower would have blown up and Gurney with it. Sewer gas, which from time to time caused the asphyxiation of sewer workers, was widely believed to be a cause of infectious disease.

There was more comedy. One day in July, Michael Faraday, dean of British chemists, had proceeded to the banks of the Thames at Hungerford, where the water was shallow and black, and ceremoniously dropped a piece of white paper in, in the presence of a coterie of reporters and spectators. The paper sank slowly and disappeared from view, the river's opacity being a measure of its pollution, according to Faraday. *Punch* was moved to comment:

> O Faraday, of Chemists,
>   The Thames we have to clear,
> The Thames, with which we slake our thirst
>   In water, or in beer.
> To take its foulness out to sea
>   Will cost the deuce knows what:
> Now in this strait can Chemistry
>   Afford us help or not? . . . .
>
> Peat charcoal is alas too dear,
>   Lime sets ammonia free.

> Chlorine—but we are talking here
>   Impertinence to thee!
> Do what thou can'st, if science can,
>   To make the River pure,
> And we shall cry, thou art the man!
>   And here's your nice manure.[18]

This was not the first time that Faraday had performed the opacity experiment. He had done it in July 1855, while traversing the river by steamboat between London and Hungerford Bridges at low water. He wrote to the *Times:*

The appearance and smell of the water forced themselves at once to my attention. The whole of the river was an opaque brown fluid. In order to test the degree of opacity, I tore up some white cards into pieces, and then moistened them, so as to make them sink easily below the surface, and then dropped some of these pieces into the water at every pier the boat came to. Before they had sunk an inch below the surface they were indistinguishable, though the sun shown brightly at the time. . . . Near the bridges the feculence rolled up in clouds so dense that they were visible at the surface even in water of this kind.[19]

This letter caused a certain amount of consternation, because Faraday was understood to believe that the "feculence" was sewage, and other chemists had to protest that the turbidity was simply the usual suspended clay and silex which, according to chemical cant, exerted a disinfecting and decomposing action on the organic matter.

Punch combined the chemists, engineers, and Goldsworthy Gurney into a fictitious "Professor Blowpipe," in a parody of the examination of technical experts by parliamentary commissions:

PROFESSOR BLOWPIPE examined. Was Professor of Chemistry in the University of Smithfield. Did not think the sewer-gases would do to light the streets with. All gas was not inflammable. Carbonic acid gas was not. It would put out fire: sulphuretted hydrogen was inflammable. Both sulphuretted hydrogen and carbonic acid gases were contained in sewers. The latter would interfere with the combustibility of the former. It was also contained in soda water.[20]

The solution finally adopted was one recommended by chemists and engineers: dumping tons of chalk lime, chloride of lime, and carbonic acid into the river to purify it. Correctly, *The Lancet* attacked this measure as only a

temporary cure or palliative. Every chemist has his own preparation of lime, of zinc, of manganese, or of charcoal for brewing his favorite sanitary soup from fetid Thames water. Meanwhile the sewers continue to discharge their putrefying noxious contents into the stream, and the main problem of drainage remains unsolved.

Lancet admitted that tossing lime into the river at the mouths of sewers abolished much of the stench. But, "how far any real sanitary good is effected by the deodorization must remain very doubtful. To deodorize is not to disinfect. . . . To destroy this stench is to remove only the warning, but too often to leave untouched the danger." Only the "total interception of the London sewage" would avail.[21]

But total interception was, of course, a political problem. In the first month of the Stink it became apparent that the government was powerless to act. On June 11, 1858, Lord John Manners, First Commissioner of Works, was questioned about any measures taken for mitigating the noisome odor. He replied that unfortunately the Thames was not in his jurisdiction. On June 15, he was questioned again on the state of the Thames and again replied that the government had nothing whatever to do with the river, that the Metropolitan Board of Works was responsible for the problem. But it was perfectly well known that the board lacked the authority and the power to collect funds for the interceptor sewer project. The Board of Works is an excellent example of the institution-generating function of environmental problems. By the terms of the Metropolis Local Management Act of 1855, the board gained limited power of administration over a considerable part of London, regardless of political boundaries. Its jurisdictional area was wholly determined by the physical disposition of sewers and drains. But because it was distinct from any city government per se, it lacked the authority to deal directly with the river, as did the government which, according to Manners, could exercise a sort of veto power over the board. The board was only given full control over metropolitan drainage in August of 1858, under the direct stimulus of the Stink.

In 1867, when the interceptor system had been completed for two years, the scientists were still wrangling over the relationship between pollution and disease. Sir John Simon, who at the beginning of his career had subscribed to the miasmatic theory, was now at the forefront of medical thought as well as of the sanitary movement. A parliamentary committee once again attempted to ascertain whether the endless stream of chemical analyses were conveying useful or valid information. Simon remarked that "the question of good supply or bad supply is not to be judged only by what the chemists from their laboratory can tell you of the water. . . . Nothing which chemists in the present state of their science can report as to their findings in London water will alter the fact of that filthy admixture." There was a present danger which was not discernible by chemists. Simon doubted that chemists could have discovered the "infectious quality" which was thought to have existed in the East London water supply during the cholera epidemic of the previous year: "I do not know that chemists could have identified it, or could have come down upon it as they would come down upon arsenic or copper. . . . We trace the sewage into the water, we trace the water to the district, and we trace the inhabitant to his cholera and death." When asked whether he could detect organic matter in water but not determine whether it bears "the germs of any particular disease," Simon replied:

Quite so. . . . The water which has done very great harm in London on various occasions, as we believe, has been water conveying what by a figure of speech I may call the actual seeds of specific disease. Chemists cannot identify those seeds. Whether microscopists can, is a question which is likely, within the course of the next twelve months, to be settled: at the present moment there is a belief amongst some very competent persons that such water would contain demonstrable microscopical organic germs, each carrying an infectious power.[22]

One chemist, Benjamin Brodie of Oxford, agreed with Simon. He refused to pronounce upon the degree to which sewage may be injurious.

That does not appear to me to be a chemical question. I think that is a question more likely to be solved by other agencies than by chemical experiments. Medical statistics will tell you more about the injurious or non-injurious character of sewage water than any analysis would do. It does not seem to me that we have . . . any accurate chemical measure of the sewage in the water; at all events, I do not know what that measure is.[23]

This statement seems to bear an implicit criticism of Frankland, who continued to insist upon the significance of the "skeleton of sewage." In the same bearing, William Miller commented that Frankland's skeleton was a figurative expression denoting the existence of nitrates and ammonia in the water. Miller noted that while Frankland summed that nitrates invariably pointed to previous contamination by sewage, recent experiments by the French agricultural chemist Jean Baptiste Boussingault had shown this not to be true.

In retrospect, this debate possesses great dramatic qualities because the physicians were already functioning within the context of the germ theory, which had yet to be proven, while the chemists and engineers were constricted by the older, miasmatic theory of contagion. The association of engineers with the old paradigm confirms Derek Price's observation that there is rarely any direct flow of information from the research front of science to that of technology, and that engineers may therefore be expected to rely upon the accrued archive of scientific knowledge.[24]

Thus engineers viewed the problem in a way that seemed irrelevant to the more advanced medical scientists like Simon. Henry Austin stated the engineers' position in 1857 when he asserted that since the courts had ruled that local authorities could not rid themselves of a nuisance by passing it on to their neighbors, "the outfall of drainage becomes at this time the great and pressing difficulty of the sanitary question; and that difficulty appears to arise mainly from the fact that the sanitary and agricultural aspects of the matter are somewhat at issue."[25] Austin had long been a booster of the agricultural use of urban sewage. Water was the best means to void noxious wastes from towns, but this mode of disposal lessened the value of the waste as manure by diluting it. To Simon, in contrast, "the only very important sanitary question . . . is the question of organic admixture."[26] Physicians were concerned with what people were ingesting, engineers with evacuation as it affected the public (more than the personal) weal and, indeed, the economy.

The Great Stink occurred at a moment when engineers were in the ascendancy in the public health movement, an ascendancy in part suggested by the sheer physical enormity of the problem and in part by a kind of stasis in medical theory while the germ theory awaited proof. So the *Times,* having long since tired of Chadwick's piecemeal approach which seemed to ignore the state of the river, sounded the keynote of public response to the Stink in calling for an engineering solution: "This is pre-eminently an iron age. . . . So we beg to suggest that a hearing be given to those engineers who propose to deal with this matter in the spirit of an iron age." Iron pipes, uniform and infinitely extensible should be laid beneath the river banks to convey the sewage away from the town. "As things are these days, this is an affair of machinery from first to last, and admits of the greatest calculation." Such an approach works for water delivery; it must also be applied to drainage.[27]

A number of conclusions regarding responses to environmental crises are evident from the experience of London during the Great Stink.

First, systemic crises invite responses, both technical and managerial, at each point in the system. Thus, household drainage, sewers, the river, main drainage, and public health were all addressed during the crisis by appropriate interest groups.

Second, the managerial response depends on crisis for its initial stimulus. The effectiveness of the solution is in part correlated with the magnitude of the crisis and in part with available technology. Technology, even if available, will not be applied without a powerful stimulus.

Third, the crisis must be perceived by those who have the power to effect amelioration, hence the symbolic significance of the Great Stink and its immediacy to the interests of parliamentarians.

Fourth, scientific response varies with disciplinary perspectives. Given a choice, that scientific analysis which accords best with the immediate aims and values of the elite will guide implementation of sanitary action, until proven wrong or insufficient. Put another way, those aims and values determine which aspect of systemic dysfunction will be attacked first. The elite, expressing its will through Parliament, would only deal with the river to seek limited goals: alleviation of the odor first and, when feasible, diversion of sewage to a site well below the city. Engineering solutions and the chemical analyses that supported them were sufficient to the cause, and medical theory had to await its day in court.

CHAPTER NINE

Environmental Crisis
and American Politics, 1860-1920

by Carl H. Moneyhon

Few people would question the proposition that a society's survival depends upon its ability to relate to the environment. The physical world provides the building blocks necessary not only for biological survival but also for development of complex social institutions typical of human life. Because of the interdependence of people and their organizations with the environment any change in the latter requires necessary alterations in the former. The dilemma posed by the relationship of men to the natural world has not generally been the survival of humans as a species, although individuals may be destroyed in the adjustment. Mankind has survived past crises. The problem has been what form society would take under different conditions.

Modern communities have been unwilling to accept naturally imposed change. More typically they have accepted the ideal that the human will can be imposed on nature. Rather than be tossed about by natural forces, peoples in the nineteenth and twentieth centuries have sought to limit or control change through the use of science, technology, and planning. We have believed that society and its values could be protected in the face of environmental change. If the status quo could not be maintained, at least destruction of the existing order could be minimized. But is such control possible? Can change be regulated for "social" purposes? The American experience in the late nineteenth century may offer us insights into dimensions of an ecological crisis for a modern community. Its response to a perceived crisis provides us with ideas about the forces that operate in a modern community to preclude or complicate a planned response.

The idea of environmental limitations on American society is not one usually associated with the country's past. The pervasive view of our national history is the story of rapid and steady expansion, of growth based upon almost infinite natural wealth. This view grew out of the colonial and early national periods when Americans felt unbounded optimism about their country and its practically limitless resources. Benjamin Franklin was typical of early observers when he noted that he believed Americans would for generations escape the constant struggle for survival that characterized European life. He believed that the American continent would provide the base for a society that would escape the pressures of population on resources that condemned the majority of peoples to mean lives. Instead of causing struggle and restrictions, the American environment would not act as a limiting factor.

This attitude persisted into the nineteenth century, expressed in popular magazines and travel literature. A typical expression was that of a visitor to the Mississippi Valley who wrote:

Our inheritance is beyond our comprehension, our climate superior, our country bounded by oceans and transversed by noble rivers and lakes. . . . Our country—the great nation—we boast of our greatness—she is emphatically the great nation. Where can we find our country's equal in geographical and natural advantages, in material progress, or in general prosperity? As a united and free people, the United States presents to the nations of the world a spectacle that we must excite the grandest wonder and admiration.[1]

And if America's possibilities amazed its inhabitants, it exercised an equally profound impact upon Europeans. They shared local wonder at the country's bounty. The possibilities afforded by the wealth of the natural environment were almost incomprehensible within the context of the European experience. In his *Democracy in America,* Alexis de Tocqueville wrote that in the struggle between men and the world that made life possible Americans had little concern for nature other than as a resource to be exploited for their benefit. He observed that they were oblivious to the awesomeness of the wild. Instead, he suggested:

[They] never think about them; they are insensible to the wonders of inanimate nature and they may be said not to perceive the mighty forests that surround them till they fall beneath the hatchet. Their eyes are fixed upon another sight: The American people views its own march across these wilds, draining swamps, turning the course of rivers, peopling solitudes, and subduing nature. This magnificent image of themselves does not meet the gaze of the Americans at intervals only; it may be said to haunt every one of them in his least as well as his most important actions and to be flitting before his mind.[2]

In short, Americans were incredibly homocentric in their approach to their surroundings. They did not see nature as a limiting force. The persistence of this view throughout the century may be seen in the writing of a British visitor to the United States, James Muirhead. In 1901 he saw the same prevailing optimism. Muirhead looked at Americans and found an "almost childlike confidence in human ability, fearlessness of both the present and future, and a sense of illimitable expansion and possibility for their country."[3]

By the middle of the nineteenth century, however, danger signals had appeared that suggested the resources necessary for a lasting and prosperous civilization were playing out. Sportsmen noticed that after several decades of commercial hunting, various forms of wildlife that had always appeared to be unlimited had begun to disappear. Herds of buffalo, which had once roamed the prairies in great numbers, were near extinction. Deer, turkey, and elk, once common throughout the United States, appeared in smaller ranges, and in settled areas they disappeared almost completely. The passenger pigeon, which had been so plentiful that they darkened the sky for days as they flew over, became extinct. On the coast, commercial fishermen witnessed a deterioration of offshore fisheries. In the 1870s, the number of fish harvested drastically declined in coastal waters and fishermen had to move into deeper waters to make their catch. This decline cut into industry profits and caused concern among fishermen who feared that the more desirable food fishes might be on the way to extinction. At the same time people in the timber industry noticed a decline in the forests, the resource that had always been considered America's richest. A paper presented to the American Association for the Advancement of Science in 1873 suggested that unless existing timber harvesting practices were halted immediately the nation's forests would be destroyed within the century. From the West, Americans received government reports that the undeveloped territories were not the promised land once supposed. John Wesley Powell's report on the western country indicated that it had great potential, but capital requirements would virtually exclude small entrepreneurs from its development. The picture was darkened even more as businessmen perceived shortages of energy and ores necessary for the industrial economy. At the turn of the century the National Conservation Commission presented evidence that indicated coal reserves, still a trillion and a half tons, would be gone by 2050 at current rates of use. It further predicted the depletion of petroleum and high-grade iron and copper ores by the same time. To cap the growing concern, the Bureau of the Census announced that the unsettled frontier on the continent no longer existed. Perhaps more than other shortages and resource problems, the end of the frontier symbolized for Americans the appearance of limits on growth.

For a society based upon growth the imposition of environmental limitations presented a terrible challenge. There would be no easy wealth to be acquired on new frontiers. Shortages, perhaps even famine, now might appear. The economy faced potential stagnation. Indeed, basic social and political values might no longer work. Frederick Jackson Turner, historian of the American frontier, warned that the country's basic democratic system of government was threatened. Turner argued that the broad distribution of political power in the United States had been made possible by the existence of free lands that gave all Americans a chance to secure a competency and economic independence. But with the disappearance of the frontier competency would no longer be possible for all. Americans in the twentieth century, he warned, faced a problem, "not to create democracy, but to conserve democratic institutions and ideals."[4] How could they protect their society in the face of changing environmental conditions?

Assessments of the proper course to take in this situation developed slowly. In addition, no single analysis emerged to gain general acceptance. Instead, the late nineteenth century saw four major ideas concerning society and environment develop, each with a wide following. These major modes of thought may be characterized as conservation, preservation, ecology, and laissez faire. While adherents to each concept recognized the general problem, their goals varied, indeed were often contradictory, and, therefore, a general reform movement to solve environmental problems was virtually impossible. Even within these groups general agreement concerning goals and means to ends proved difficult. For Americans, therefore, there was a general perception of a crisis, but little agreement on its definition or on measures to alleviate it.

Of the four major ideologies, conservationism received the greatest publicity during this period. Its spokesmen were the most vocal and political. The concept promised to meet the crisis with minimal modification of existing American society. Conservationists emphasized the role of scientific and rational institutions in achieving a solution. Proper application of these techniques, they believed, would abate the problem by providing new resources to avoid shortages and making more efficient use of the natural wealth that was already available. This particular approach found its strongest adherents among scientists, professionals such as physicians and scholars, and some industrialists—men who possessed the technical knowledge that they believed would save the nation. Elements of conservationist thought were found in a host of programs developed during the late nineteenth century. Typical was the effort of Bernhard E. Fernow and Gifford Pinchot to bring scientific methods of tree farming into currency in the timber industry. Through careful cultivation, development of new kinds of timber, and proper harvesting, they believed the nation's timber resources could be preserved practically intact for future generations as well as the current. Perhaps no better statement exists of the kind of thought that embraced the conservationists than that of the economist Simon Patten. In *The New Basis of Civilization* he indicated his belief that science and technology would provide the ultimate means for man to overcome the limits of environment. He wrote:

Artificial culture and experimental science have already fundamentally altered the elemental relations existing two hundred years ago between population and environment. Yet to say that the methods which have made man physically independent of the local food supply are artificial is to underrate the powers of the new forces by implying that they are constantly opposed by fundamental natural forces which in the end must again triumph. The final victory of man's machinery over nature's materials is the next logical process in evolution, as nature's control of human society was the transition from anarchic and puny individualism to the group acting as a powerful, intelligent organism. Machinery, science, and intelligence moving on the face of the other may well affect it as the elements do, upbuilding, obliterating, and creating; but they are man's forces and will be used to hasten his dominion over nature.[5]

The conservationists believed that promised shortages could be avoided, that the social status quo could consequently be maintained, with the innovation made possible by science and technology.

As a practical program, a variety of governmental agencies designed to apply the conservationist solution to problems appeared after the 1870s. The first of these was the United States Fish Commission created in 1871. Congress created it specifically to discover what was happening to the coastal fisheries and what might be done to prevent their destruction. Its first commissioner, Spencer Fullerton Baird, was a scientist who pushed the commission into a general study of marine biology and fish culture. As a result of these studies, Congress funded programs to replenish fish stocks and also moved to restrict fishing. Conservationism was also apparent in the work of the Division of Forestry created in 1881 within the Department of Agriculture. Under Franklin B. Hough, Bernhard E. Fernow, and Gifford Pinchot the division collected information on scientific tree culture and disseminated that information throughout the United States. At the request of the nation's chief foresters, Congress passed laws to preserve timber resources. Typical of these was the 1891 legislation allowing the president to set aside parts of the public domain for forest reserves. The most encompassing legislation passed through Congress in 1897, and authorized a system of management for these national forests under the direction of the Department of the Interior.

By 1900, however, conservationists confronted a dilemma. Their piecemeal approach to conservation provided only limited results. While they could respond to problems as they arose, the number of crisis situations continued to mount. Further, they became aware of the interrelationship of environmental problems. Realizing that the situation required a broad approach, conservationists, encouraged by the leadership of President Theodore Roosevelt, attempted to expand their ideal into a general reform. Roosevelt became the center of this movement when he brought to his administration prominent advocates of conservation, such as Gifford Pinchot, W. J. McGee, and Charles Van Hise. In 1908 the president called together a conference of governors to secure broad support for various conservation measures that he hoped to push through Congress. The general thrust of these measures would be to create a general conservation policy, the first step of which would be the organization of a National Conservation Commission to inventory resources that would allow better planning. Roosevelt further envisioned annual conservation conferences in Washington to help develop a broad national policy. Emphasizing his concern, Roosevelt told the assembled governors that the conservation of natural resources was "the weightiest problem now before the Nation." He warned them that without quick measures, the nation's natural wealth was "in danger of exhaustion."[6]

What would a general conservation policy have involved? Since one was not implemented it is difficult to say. However, some insight into the possibilities may be gained from an examination of

Charles Van Hise's *The Conservation of Natural Resources*. Van Hise was a geographer at the University of Wisconsin, a prominent advisor to Roosevelt on conservation matters. His study appeared after the meeting of the North American Conservation Conference in 1909 and proposed a general attack upon the problem of wasted resources, the waste not only of material but also human wealth. Van Hise believed that the most pressing problem was the exhaustion of fossil fuels and metal ores, and he urged as a solution the creation of more efficient methods of using these resources and greater efficiency in using their products. In addition he suggested that science's resources had to be directed toward the development of a more efficient technology and also to the discovery of alternative sources of power and raw materials. But Van Hise also thought a human dimension existed in the crisis. He feared that depletion of resources and the growing pollution produced by industrialization threatened the quality of life for most Americans. Here again he advised the application of science. Scientific medicine and public health, for example, could make possible a quality of life in an environment that might previously have killed people. Of course people complicated the situation by their reproduction. Van Hise urged that people be managed in much the same way as other resources, even advocating the application of knowledge gained from stock breeding to human populations so that planned rather than prolific procreation might be achieved.

The move to a general policy split the conservationists for development of a program raised major questions as to means and ends. All could agree that the environment must be managed, but they could not agree as to who should do the managing and whose purpose should be served by it. In short, there was no agreement as to who constituted society or what defined social interest. As a result two major groups emerged among the conservationists. The first, consisting of Roosevelt, Pinchot, Van Hise and others, came to believe that planning and definition must be in the hands of society through government. The second pushed the view that the response must be by society through individuals and private interests of the community. As a result, the conservationists, even though they agreed on the nature of the environmental problem and the solution to the problem, split over the question of social welfare.

The conservationist tradition developed by Roosevelt and his followers represented a marked challenge to many traditional American values, although it reaffirmed others. In the case of the latter it pronounced the soundness of the egalitarian concepts that had typified the American ideology. Pinchot argued that natural resources had to be developed and utilized for the use of the many, not the profit of a few. W. J. McGee, another of Roosevelt's advisors, expanded this view when he provided a definition of the ethical doctrine he believed should typify conservation. It should involve, he believed,

a nobler patriotism, under which citizen-electors will cleave more strongly to their birthright of independence and strive more vigorously for purity of the ballot, for rightness in laws, for cleanness in courts, and for forthrightness in administration; by a higher honesty of purpose between man and man; by a warmer charity, under which the good of all will more fairly merge with the good of each; by a stronger family sense, tending toward a realization of the rights of the unborn; by a deeper probity, maturing in the realizing sense that each holder of the sources of life is but a trustee for his nominal possessions, and is responsible to all men, and for all time for making the best use of them in the common interest; and by a livelier humanity, in which each will feel that he lives not for himself alone but as a part of a common life for a common world and for the common good.[7]

The concept suggested by McGee and the others promised a better life for the individual, but it also hypothesized a national or social interest within which the individual's well-being could be secured. Government would be the mechanism through which the broader interests of the community would be enforced and defined.

In proposing a greater role for government in ordering society's relationship to the environment, these conservationists attacked two major concepts: individualism and laissez faire. They particularly singled out individualism as an archaic idea that worked well within a boundless society but worked to the disadvantage of society as a whole in a limited community. Laissez faire was simply the means through which individualism was allowed to run rampant. McGee condemned the two as major producers of waste throughout the history of the nation. He concluded:

In all the world's history no other such saturnalia of squandering the sources of permanent prosperity was ever witnessed! In the material aspect, our individual liberty became collective license; the balance between impulse and responsibility was lost, the future of the people and the Nation was forgotten, and the very name of posterity was made a by-word by men in high places; and worst of all the very profligacies came to be venerated as law and even crystalized foolishly in decisions or more questionably in enactments—and for long they were not to stand in the way of the growing avalanche of extravagance.[8]

Such individualism was no longer possible, indeed it was dangerous, and Van Hise reiterated the theme of the Roosevelt conservationists when he urged its abandonment. "He who thinks not of himself primarily, but of his race, and of its future," he wrote, "is the new patriot."[9]

The attack upon such cherished traditions and on the interests supported by them quickly promoted a response. Hostility toward the idea of government planning had always existed within the movement; now it became a revolt against the president's leadership. We can see the idea that planned response should be in the hands of individuals and private enterprise rather than the government in the proposals of John W. Powell for the western lands that he published in 1890. Powell believed that it would be tempting to allow the government to establish control over development there, but he argued against it. Rather, he urged that government confine itself strictly to the development of water resources in the area and the provision of a legal framework for their effective and efficient utilization. Once the ground rules had been provided, free enterprise should be allowed to enter the field. Laborers should employ themselves and those with the genius to organize the endeavor should control the land. The money for development should come from private enterprise. After establishing the framework, he advised, "I say to government, Hands Off!"[10]

After the introduction of Roosevelt's ideas for general conservation reform, the opposition to government planning expanded. At the National Conference of Governors in 1908, Edmund J. James, representing Illinois, attacked the conference's organizers for putting too much emphasis upon the destruction of resources and exaggerating that facet of the problem. He believed more attention needed to be paid to the development of replacement resources. But his primary concern was that the conference's focus was being used to persuade the American people to adopt unnecessarily restrictive governmental policies. The result, he believed, would be the stifling of genius that had made possible many of the country's greatest advances in mining and agriculture. James revealed a general distrust of the idea of government intervention and restriction. That inability to decide who should provide planning, who should decide the social good, made a common approach to the crisis practically impossible. The power of those opposed to the intervention of the national government was finally felt when William Howard Taft became president. Taft proved reluctant to push forward the power of the nation at the expense of individuals or states. In the end the schism made a general national policy untenable.

Divisions within the conservationist camp created problems, and these were further complicated by the opposition of people who saw the crisis but had an alternative solution—the preservationists. This group represented a large number of Americans who viewed the environment somewhat romantically. Some were outright reactionaries. They believed that physical development did not always lead to progress. They argued that the best in life might be found in nature rather than in the words of man. Preservationism was not a new idea in the United States; in fact, it had a long tradition that could be traced in the ideas of Thoreau, George Catlin, and others. By the late nineteenth century men like Frederick Law Olmsted, Charles W. Eliot, and John Muir had become its carriers. They believed that nature possessed a spiritual quality necessary for the survival of mankind and argued for wilderness, for the preservation of the undeveloped. Muir wrote, "Everybody needs beauty as well as bread, places to play in and pray in, where nature may heal and cheer and give strength to body and soul alike." Eliot, president of Harvard and chairman of the National Conservation Congress in 1909, cooperated with the conservationists but believed nature was more than a resource for human utilization; it was worth preserving for itself. To him the city and the factory system created evils too great for the human body to endure and which only a resort to nature could cure. Frederick Law Olmsted, whose career included laying out natural sanctuaries in the heart of cities, suggested that the contemplation of nature was necessary for the health and vigor of mankind. Without it man had, "softening of the brain, paralysis, palsy, monomania, insanity, mental and nervous excitability, moroseness, melancholy or irascibility, and incapacitation of the individual for proper exercise of intellectual and moral forces."[11]

The preservationists' position was not an easy one for an individual at the turn of the century. To adopt it usually involved serious problems, for many could appreciate the advantages made possible by urban and industrial civilization. Yet at the same time they feared it and looked to the past, to a natural order for solace in the face of the upheaval of the industrial age. The paradoxes involved in the preservationist view appear prominently in the thought of John Burroughs. In *The Summit of the Year* he criticized the conservationist approach, the scientific way of looking at the world. It provided a mixed blessing:

Well, we can gain a lot of facts, such as they are, but we may lose our own souls. This spirit has invaded school and college. Our young people go to the woods with pencil and note-book in hand; they drive sharp bargains with every flower and bird and tree they meet; they want tangible assets that can be put down in black and white. Nature as a living joy, something to love, to live with, to brood over, is now, I fear, seldom thought of. It is only a mine to be worked and to be through with, a stream to be fished, a tree to be shaken, a field to be gleaned. With what desperate thoroughness the new men study the birds; and about all their studies yield is a mass of dry, unrelated facts.[12]

However, Burroughs could not see a way out of the dilemma. He did not like what was happening, but he did not believe the world could forget what it had now learned. He concluded that men ultimately "must face and accept the new situation. . . . We shall write less poetry, but we ought to live saner lives; we shall tremble and worship less, but we shall be more at home in the universe."[13] All preservationists were not as willing as Burroughs to accept compromise with "progress." In political battles of the Roosevelt and Taft years they would frequently stand against the conservationists and their opposition, as the internal split within conservationism, would work to preclude the development of a broad approach to ecological crisis.

A third approach to the apparent crisis of the late nineteenth century embraced elements and values of both conservationism and preservationism but had its unique elements. Its uniqueness would make its adherents uncooperative with those of the other two ideas. This approach may be called ecological. The concept of ecology involved the idea that man was integrally involved with nature in an interdependent relationship. Ecologists, therefore, argued that the demands of nature must play as great a role in determining a proper course for society to follow as the needs of man. The earliest spokesman for this view in the United States was George P. Marsh, a diplomat who had served in Europe and witnessed first-hand the devastation that resulted from ignoring the demands of nature. In 1864 he published *Man and Nature* in which he warned Americans that they were creating problems for themselves by destroying their environment and cautioned them not to interfere with the "spontaneous arrangements of the organic and inorganic world." Marsh believed that nature possessed a natural balance and that man, if he dealt unknowingly with it, could destroy that balance and make the world unfit for life. Looking at what Italians had done to their mountains, the destruction of timber and the resulting erosion and flooding, Marsh saw ample proof of his view's validity. He told Americans that they must stop. "We are even now breaking up the floor and wainscoting and doors and window frames of our dwelling, for fuel to warm our bodies and to seethe our pottage, and the world cannot afford to wait till the slow and sure progress of exact science has taught it better economy."[14]

Marsh presented a strong challenge to the entire American concept of life and nature. He suggested that man might not have the right to do with nature what he wanted but rather that he needed to understand what nature wanted. Perhaps it was too radical a departure for the time; consequently its adherents remained a small group, generally confined to the academy. Still, it was a point of view important among a potentially influential group of people. Unfortunately, it provided another approach to the American environmental problem and thus fragmented social response. The ecologists, because of their definition of the problem, had to move slowly. They had to discover what the correct relationship with the world should be. Nathaniel Shaler argued for education, for only through the study of nature would an answer to environmental problems be discovered. Shaler, however, found this goal hindered by the very institutions designed for study. He wrote of scientific education in the United States:

We now present the realm to beginners as a group of fragments labeled astronomy, geology, chemistry, physics, and biology, each, as set forth, appearing to him as a little world in itself, with its own separate life, having little to do with its neighbors. It is rare, indeed, in a very considerable experience with youths to find one who has gained any inkling as to the complete unity of nature. Seldom it is, even with those who attain mastery in some one of these learnings, that we find a true sense as to the absolute oneness of the realm, or the place of man as the highest product of its work.[15]

The ecologists perceived themselves in an adversary relationship with the rest of the community, including conservationists and preservationists, and believed that they had the only answer to the situation.

But if the ecologists felt they had the truth, to outsiders this particular approach must have bordered on heresy. It attacked not only traditional religious views but basic ideas about life. Edward Evans categorized the points of conflict between the ecologists and traditional society: they challenged the Judaic and Christian views of man's dominant position in the world; they attacked man's conceit, his belief in himself as the lord of creation; and they criticized man's relationship to the plants and animals around him which he had too readily destroyed for his own convenience. Instead, the ecologists proposed a new relationship. The horticulturalist Liberty Hyde Bailey summarized the ecological approach in *The Holy Earth* when he wrote:

A constructive and careful handling of the resources of the earth is impossible except on a basis of large cooperation and of association for mutual welfare. The great inventions and discoveries of recent time have extensive social significance.

Yet we have other relations than with the physical and static materials. We are parts in a living, sensitive creation. The theme of evolution has overturned our attitude toward this creation. The living creation is not exclusively man-centered: it is biocentric.[16]

Conservationism, preservationism, and ecology represented activist approaches to environmental pressures. A fourth approach was the adoption of a wait-and-see attitude, a belief in laissez faire—let the situation develop and find out what happens. Accompanying this point of view was a basic optimism, a trust that nature or God would work things out. Its exponents adopted basic hostility toward those groups seeking to intervene in the process. George L. Knapp condemned the conservationists as "unadulterated humbugs" who sought to undermine the best in American life. In an article for the *North American Review* he wrote:

That the modern Jeremiahs are as sincere as was the older one I do not question. But I count their prophesies to be baseless vaporings, and their vaunted remedy worse than the fancied disease. I am one who can see no warrant of law, or justice, nor of necessity for that wholesale reversal of our traditional policy which the advocates of "conservation" demand. I am one who does not shiver for the future at the sight of a load of coal, nor view a steel-mill as the arch-robber of posterity.[17]

While there might be immediate shortages, existing institutions would meet the crisis. The optimism of the advocates of laissez faire was strikingly expounded by Congressman Martin Dies of Texas before Congress on August 30, 1913. Dies strongly opposed efforts to prevent the construction of a dam across the Hetch Hetchy Valley in California, and speaking to the point he said:

I sympathize with my friends in California who want to take a part of the public domain now. . . . I am willing to let them have it.

That is what the great resources of this country are for. They are for the American people. I want them to open the coal mines in Alaska. I want them to open the reservations of this country. I am not for preservations or parks. I would have the great timber and mineral and coal resources of this country opened to the people . . . Let California have it, and let Alaska open her coal mines. God Almighty has located the resources of this country in such form as that His children will not use them in disproportion, and your Pinchots will not be able to controvert and circumvent the laws of God Almighty.[18]

The ideology of the advocates of laissez faire appear clearly in the statements of both Knapp and Dies. It represented, at least in part, a reassertion of two traditional American ideas. The environment existed for man to subdue and develop, and to be subdued and developed by private initiative, by the individual whose pursuit of his own interests worked in the interest of the American people. In addition, God had a special concern with the people of the United States, and he would not allow anything bad to happen. While a crisis might exist, there was no need to change American ways.

Resources were diminishing. Wild life was disappearing. Everybody could see that something was happening. Something had gone wrong. But no consensus emerged as to what should be done. If planning was to be done, who would be responsible? If technological innovation was necessary, who would sponsor it? What approach should be taken? The problem raised by the crisis was no longer one of science. What had emerged was a political dilemma in which a variety of views contested for acceptance and no one could claim majority support. Everyone claimed to speak for public interest, for the national good and welfare, but the various groups proposing solutions offered different definitions of both the public interest and how to secure it. Consequently, reform efforts ran into trouble in the national political arena. In one episode after another environmental reformers found themselves unable to cooperate with one another. As a result, perhaps, the forces for laissez faire won the day. It was better not to change than to move into areas that even the experts could not agree about. During Roosevelt's administration measures went to Congress proposing national planning. Each was rebuffed. When the president created the Inland Waterways Commission to develop a comprehensive plan to merge local water projects into a national program, state and local opposition built up enough opposition in Congress to defeat it. Private interests in the western states achieved the removal of Frederick H. Newell from the Bureau of Reclamation after Newell attempted to use the powers granted in the Newlands Act to take federal revenues derived from the sale and rental of western lands and put them into the construction of federal dams and reservoirs. Newell's transgression was interference with local individual rights and economic opportunities. The government proved more responsive to strong private interests than to a theoretical national concern which lacked clear definition or articulation. Individuals could demand legislative action, the nation and the future had little voice.

While Roosevelt fought battles with the forces hostile to an active response to the crisis, he also had to fight with other activists. It was a struggle that was suicidal and that polarized opinions rather than forging a synthetic view. In 1909, conservationists split into public and private planning groups when President Taft named Richard A. Ballinger to head the Department of the Interior. Ballinger favored local and private development of resources over federal. Subsequently he loosened federal controls over these operations and restored public lands to the private sector for the development of power sites. Ballinger's efforts provoked a struggle between him and the Roosevelt conservationists. The specific issue was a problem of conflict of interest in the disposition of Alaskan coal lands, but it must also be seen as one over basic approach. Indicative of the broader nature of the conflict was the general attack following the Ballinger affair upon Roosevelt's supporters in the government. Taft complained of the "jesuit guile" used by Chief Forester Gifford Pinchot in undermining Ballinger, and ultimately even Pinchot, the most powerful of the Roosevelt conservationists, was removed from office. Politically the battle was a disaster for Taft, but for conservation it was also a tragedy. The struggle over Ballinger split conservationists into two uncooperative camps and ended efforts to secure joint action from them.

While the conservationists fought one another they also encountered the opposition of the preservationists. In 1913 they split over the development of the Hetch Hetchy Valley, a battle won by the former but which worked to worsen relations between the two groups. When the City of San Francisco sought to create a reservoir within the boundaries of Yosemite National Park, the preservationists, led by John Muir, worked to stop it. Muir condemned those who would destroy the natural beauty of the valley. "Dam Hetch Hetchy!" he wrote, "As well dam for water-tanks the people's cathedrals and churches, for no holier temple has ever been consecrated by the heart of man."[19] The conservationists, however, argued in favor of the reservoir. In the end the dam was built, but preservationists and conservationists had demonstrated their lack of common goals or an ability to cooperate.

What was the result? No broad reform plan emerged, no directed solution to the problem. Instead the nation met crises as it had in the past, piecemeal and responsively. This placed adjustments in each case in the hands of those directly tied to specific shortages. Thus, power companies developed waterways, steel companies sought new sources of iron ore, and so on. In the short run this probably averted the crisis. Private industry and enterprise was interested in efficient utilization of resources. It also managed to develop alternative sources for the energy and raw materials whose destruction had been feared.

But in the long run what took place? The discovery of new sources of diminishing materials spurred American growth, and the American population quickly expanded to consume whatever could be produced. Thus, society was still tied to the same pattern of utilization of resources that had created the initial crisis. That portion of the problem had only been delayed. However, in addition the crisis had prompted less visible change in the American community. The status quo had not been maintained; change had not been stopped. In fact, Americans confronted the very crisis feared by Frederick Jackson Turner. By the success they achieved in solving the immediate problems, private entrepreneurs secured greater control over the resources that they needed and, consequently, greater economic and political power. Within this situation the chance of the individual either to gain economic power or exercise power outside of these corporations was diminished. The crisis forced change, whether Americans planned for it or not.

CHAPTER TEN

Ecology, Economics, and the Quality of Life

by John M. Culbertson

Some important lessons about the state of humanity seem to be illuminated by parallels between economics and ecology. In both the management of economics and the management of the natural habitat we now face complex and dangerous problems. Moreover, the subjects of ecology and economics, if developed scientifically, would show many similarities. However, in both areas, valid knowledge must compete with ideology, and scientific work with the projection onto the subject of ideologies. The versions of economics that have dominated attention for the past two centuries, indeed, were the shadows of ideologies rather than realistic characterizations of how economics work. The discussions and conflicts that determine policies and actions toward the economy and the environment seem to be increasingly ideologized and to have now little place for objective knowledge and analysis. The projection of ideology into interpretations of evolution, the basic framework of the life sciences, seems on the rise in recent years.

It would be pleasant to recount a story of how improving knowledge was being applied with increasing precision to protecting and enhancing man's natural habitat, but the true story may prove to be the opposite one: irrational and unrealistic group ideologies dominating policies concerning the economy and the environment, completing the ideologization of academic theories in these areas, and driving knowledge and reason from the stage of human endeavors.

Basic questions thus exist as to our ability to improve, or even to maintain, the quality of the habitat and of human life.

To begin with, in both economics and ecology, that is, in the management of our economies and of our natural habitat, the world now faces problems that seem very difficult, new, even unprecedented, and threatening if not managed successfully. The problems facing us in the management of our natural habitat outreach our knowledge. What effect will oil spills have on the organisms at the base of the food chain leading to the world's essential supply of seafoods? How will actions possibly disrupting the ozone layer and air pollution from the burning of fossil fuels affect the earth's absorption of energy, its temperature, and its life processes? What will be the outcome of the accumulation of radioactive wastes from atomic power plants?

Solid answers are not available, not even from the best informed experts, nor will they necessarily be in the future. Yet the stakes here are high. The failure that is now within man's power is far greater than what lay in the hands of earlier generations.

New technical knowledge has been a potent creator of new problems. The kinds of knowledge that would help in handling these new problems have not come wrapped in the same package with the knowledge that caused them. And if the relevant knowledge did, in some sense, exist, should we have the capability of using it? Suppose the truth were that the safety of civilization required banning SSTs, aerosol cans, the carrying of oil by tankers, and sharply curtailing the burning of fossil fuels. Should we believe the expert who told us so? Surely there would be other experts with more pleasant predictions. Would not the more optimistic story win popular acceptance?

In managing economics we also face pressing new problems which in a sense parallel those relating to the environment. Most nations confront worsening inflation, economic conflict, and groups subject to large unemployment. Existing political arrangements may have little tolerance for worsening inflation, continued high unemployment, and strike-caused disruption. Political unrest or dissension caused by the problems, however, will worsen them, creating a vicious circle. Here is an explosive situation, one with a fuse shorter than that of our environmental problems.

Is there in this case also a lack of needed knowledge? Are the cures for these economic problems known? Of course, there is no lack of proferred remedies. But the remedies—and the factions sponsoring them—are in conflict with one another. Each group seems to prefer the remedy that lays the blame, and the burden, on others.

But suppose the true answer to achieve price stability with full employment and a reasonable pattern of incomes requires removing the existing powers of occupational groups to compete against one another in demanding increases in their money incomes and other privileges. Perhaps it is not difficult to believe that such is at least a part of the true answer. What government could act on this truth? What government could take the actions that would prevent occupational groups from demanding and receiving more than is consistent with full employment, price stability, and a reasonable pattern of incomes?

The problems posed by the prevailing arrangements for setting incomes and prices were created not by advances in technology but by supposed advances in social policy and legislation, by what was billed as "reform." But having thus created the new situation, have we the capability of dealing with it?

Similarly, the great strides made in transportation and communications in recent decades and the related development of multinational corporations have created a new potential for worldwide economic integration. The supposedly enlightened view has been that this tide of change is only another manifestation of progress, it being taken for granted that the activities in question, like other economic activities, are automatically self-regulating, governed "as if by an invisible hand." But, as the internationalization of economic activities undercuts the powers of national governments, as we observe the realities of international competition based on low wage rates and lax standards of environmental protection, can we maintain faith in this ancient metaphor? Does the invisible hand also take care of the world population problem? Of the destruction of land from overuse deriving from overpopulation? Does it regulate the creation of pollutants and the composition of the earth's upper atmosphere? Once admitted, a questioning of faith in the automaticity and self-directing nature of progress finds much to question.

So some parallels. We confront serious problems in managing our economies and our habitat. The problems were created by—well, let us say, progress. In both areas, no solution to the problems is in view. In both areas, dealing with the problems involves managing the performance of very complex systems. Thus, it requires knowledge; just the right actions must be taken. A symbolic gesture, a new slogan, the striking of a public-relations posture, the creation of an appealing scapegoat will not suffice. But both areas are battle-grounds of group beliefs and ideologies. Under these conditions, can true knowledge be distinguished from the obviously abundant false knowledge? Will increasing ideologization of academic work virtu-ally eliminate true knowledge? And, in either case, if true knowledge were somehow identified, are existing governments capable of act-ing on it?

How did we get into this situation? When the actions were being taken and the laws were being passed that created it, what was supposed to take care of these problems?

There is a simple and illuminating answer to this question. Such difficulties were supposed to be taken care of by progress, by the invisible hand that guides progress. That is to say, the era of enthusiastic and thoughtless change has been an era of faith in the superintendence of man's mundane affairs by a beneficent provi-dence. After all, the implicit reasoning goes, if it is the natural lot of man to progress, to move onward and upward, then the changes that seem naturally to occur or to reflect "reforms" must be such progress. If, indeed, this is *progress*, it is superfluous to ask whether it is desirable.

So onward! Change is progress—or it would not occur. These ideas are hardly unfamiliar to us, for they still rule our world. The enthusiasm for accelerating change, unplanned, directed by no knowledge, free of all guidance; the faith that things cannot turn out badly, that if progress causes problems more progress will cure the problems; the ideas and actions that created our hazardous position in relation to our natural habitat and in relation to one another in our conflict-ridden economies—these arise from this providentialist ideology, from the faith in a man-centered, progress-granting uni-verse. This providentialism is the dominating belief of recent cen-turies. It is, if one will, the new superstition of the modern world.

Humanity has not always lived in the world of this ideology. Indeed, such conceptions would have been incomprehensible to the ancient world, the medieval world, or the civilizations of the Orient. This providentialist ideology has been dominant for only the past two centuries. Indeed, we might say we have just celebrated the bicentennial not only of the United States but also of the reign of its ideology of providentialist individualism, of faith in the "invisible hand." For 1776 was the birthday not only of our Declaration of Independence but also of the publication of Adam Smith's *Wealth of Nations*.

The basic story of Adam Smith's new view of the economy and

the world of human affairs is this. Our world, our universe, is a simple, mechanical contrivance. Newton demonstrated this—if we extrapolate to human affairs his conception of the universal law of gravitation and the uniform motion of the planets. Behind its seeming complexity, in this new view, the whole world is governed by such simple, mechanical, and universal laws. These laws comprise a grand design, a universal plan. They are harmonious and designed with man as the beneficiary. Man has only to act out his passive, mechanical role, must not presume to contribute to the process with morality, wisdom, or virtue. Man's earlier efforts to develop civilized patterns of life, to elevate humanity by religion and frameworks of morality, of social conceptions of virtue, the planning and guidance of nations by monarchs and their ministers, all this was a mistake, an intrusion into the domain of the invisible hand, a violation of the rule, laissez faire. In relation to the thought and experience of all man's earlier civilizations, this was radical doctrine.

To fit this pattern, people must be asserted to behave rather like Newton's planets: simply, with no role for culture and group processes, exhibiting a universal arithmetic. Corresponding to Newton's universal principle of attraction of matter is an asserted universal desire of people to fill built-in economic wants. The selfish actions of asocial individuals, thus, form a pre-programmed pattern as exact and as naturally harmonious as do the motions of the planets. The only hazard is that, failing to perceive the majestic harmony hidden behind the clutter of everyday events, we shall spoil this grand design by our well-intentioned but superfluous and foolish meddling.

Do these doctrines convey knowledge about the way things are? Or are they the projection into events of an ideology? Do they characterize the way the performance of economics is determined by their structures and processes? Or are they justificatory propaganda for the political faction with which Smith associated himself; Whig, anti-monarchist, Protestant, individualistic, pro-business, anti-aristocratic, anti-clerical?

Smith's doctrines served his cause. Virtue and morality must be de-emphasized so business can free itself from moral standards defined by the Church or the government. Planning, guidance of events on behalf of society and civilized standards, knowledge, wisdom must be depicted as superfluous, for the monarch and his ministers were the presumed providers of these. A minimal role of government suited the special desires of Smith's Scots, who felt themselves further from the throne and the British Parliament than their English competitors. The doctrine that selfishness is the agent of Providence and that one best benefits his fellow man by enriching himself surely fell like music on the ears of the members of the rising business class. Was the justification provided by Smith's doctrines for the causes and the group interests with which he associated himself an accident?

Despite the continued rationalization of it by conventional economics, the Smithian world view, it seems, cannot be taken seriously as naturalistic knowledge. Its natural harmony, its invisible hand, its universally beneficent competition are not characteristics of the world, reflecting identifiable structures and processes, consistently confirmed by experience. Rather, the Smithian story is a new kind of myth, a secular, mechanistic myth which supports a political ideology. The new view rose to dominate not because of its truth-value and surely not because of persuasive support within a rigorous methodology but because the groups and interests it served rose to dominance. It is this that made the doctrines "plausible" and elevated to positions of influence those who saw the world in this way.

While this world view has been dominant now for nearly two centuries, especially in Great Britain and the United States, there always have been those who rejected it in its entirety and offered quite different world views. In 1767, Adam Smith's contemporary, Sir James Steuart, published a version of economics that was virtually the opposite of Smith's. Neither providentialistic, individualistic, nor mechanistic, his economics depicted man as a social being, the nation as the major organizing and planning agency of the existing world, and the success of a society as depending on the knowledge and wisdom provided in the shaping of its institutions and policies. A number of versions of non-natural-harmony economics have been developed, and, in some times and places, have been influential. But the period since World War II, and yet further the past decade, have seen an extraordinary further swing toward the ideology of providentialist individualism.

The dominance of the Smithian economics of providentialist individualism relate to ecology and the natural habitat in two ways. First, the exploitive, every-man-for-his-own-fast-buck attitude that prevailed toward the habitat in the United States derived from the world view for which this economics provided the central core. The invisible hand was assumed to take care of the land, the buffalo, and the Indians along with its other duties. Government management or regulation of land and resources was inconsistent with a dominant world view in which management and regulation were undesirable. Economic beliefs and ideology, in other words, dominated the way the land and natural resources were treated.

Second, the intellectual tide from which ecology developed, largely in recent decades, is quite at variance with that exemplified by Smithian economics. It explained the development of species—ultimately, the world of living systems—in terms of natural structures and processes; it was not anthropocentric or providentialist. The theory of natural selection showed how complex living systems could come into being, change, and develop through a process which reflected only the behavior of matter. The argument from design—"there is order, therefore there must be a man-like planner of the order"—that implicitly underlay most of earlier Western thought now had a viable competitor. A basis now existed for naturalistic thought and knowledge regarding living systems.

The new Darwinian life sciences, interpreting nature in terms of the behavior of matter in its various structures and processes, went from success to success. Biology, genetics, microbiology, and ecology discovered and systematically explained new worlds that could not have been made meaningful within the old framework. Moreover, the biologists searching for the structures and processes that cause particular behavior, by following reasoned rules of investigation and discourse, could largely agree as to the explanation.[1]

In comparison, it becomes clear that the providentialist doctrines do not convey knowledge about the world but reflect the human imagination, human wishes and conceits, and human group conflicts. Each tells a story that justifies the beliefs or the actions of some group. The Smithians say Providence designed the universe for individualism; the Marxists say Providence set it up for man to progress through conflict to a cleansed proletarian anarchism featuring a New Man; the anarchists say that simply abolishing government will bring Utopia. In what ways are the credentials of these secular prophets superior to those of the many varieties of prophets who claim to speak directly to God or to *be* God? Is not asserting that individualism (or revolution, or the abolition of government) will bring an ideal world—in the absence of any naturalistic explanation of structures and processes that could possibly lead to such an outcome and in the face of so much contrary experience—supernaturalistic? Is it not, in effect, a claimed miracle? Are inexplicable wonders provided by an invisible hand, by natural harmony, by "competition" any less miraculous or supernaturalistic than such inexplicable wonders issuing from Zeus, nature spirits, or the doctrines of witchcraft or astrology?

Thus ecology, as a Darwinian science, and the prevailing economics, as a projection of the ideology of providentialist individualism, belong to two very different realms of discourse. One is devoted to representing nature's structures and processes, to representing things as they are. The other has little relation to actual structures and processes or to the pattern of actual events. It entails the imaginative use of language, the creation of imaginary entities which serve as "explanations," the construction of hypothetical cases and "models" which serve in the place of actual causal mechanisms.

It is interesting to observe that present-day discourse and beliefs on natural events rather broadly can be divided into these two realms. One is practical, realistic, down-to-earth, governed by experience or by success and failure; it demonstrates real skill and achievement in managing events. The other is a domain of words tied not to events and realities but to image making, persuasion, group conflicts and group ideologies; this is a realm of great pretensions and claims but of little achievement in managing events. Ecology and economics, in this interpretation, exemplify these two domains.

The public debate over environmental issues has come to fall conspicuously into the domain of ideology and propaganda, the domain within which economic issues long have been dealt with. Organized groups actively participating in these debates do not exemplify an open-minded search for knowledge and its reasoned application to policy choices. Rather, the groups represent ideological postures suiting the tastes and interests of various constituencies. The groups war against one another in the realm of imaginative use of language and symbols—an ever-popular human activity.

As background for the momentous habitat-affecting decisions and actions of coming decades, it is important to understand past developments in this area, what might have been done that was not, and the dominant role of ideology as a shaper of ideas and events. The nineteenth century featured a pervasive contest between policies based on the ideology for providentialist individualism and others based on an asserted need for positive action by government to guide events and maintain civilized standards. The British "factory legislation" of the early 1800s, for example, exemplified a victory of the positive-government approach over the earlier laissez faire approach.

In the same period, the United States made a spectacular leap in the opposite direction. The program proposed to the nation by President John Quincy Adams reflected an explicit effort to use applied science for the advancement of the people of the United States and ultimately of humanity in general. Adams also proposed active support by the nation of further development of knowledge.

The cornerstone of Adams's program was his plan to use the public lands as the means by which the United States could break a path to a higher quality of life—raising issues which have their present-day parallels:

The public lands are the richest inheritance ever bestowed by a bountiful Creator upon any national community. . . . I had long entertained and cherished the hope that these public lands were among the chosen instruments of Almighty power . . . of improving the condition of man, by establishing the practical, self-evident truth of the natural equality and brotherhood of all mankind, as the foundation of all human government, and by banishing slavery and war from the earth.

Compared to what might have been done, the actual outcome was tragic. The fateful choice was implicit in the nation's preference for Andrew Jackson over Adams. The decisive actions were initiated, in Adams's words, by "the project first proclaimed by Andrew Jackson . . . of giving away the national inheritance to private land jobbers, or to the states in which they lie."[2] As a result, "the American Union, as a moral person in the family of nations, is to live from hand to mouth, and to cast away instead of using for the improvement of its own condition, the bounties of Providence."[3]

The use to be made of the public lands was not an isolated issue. Within the surging ideology of providentialist individualism, which buried Adams and his program, it was linked to the protection and humane treatment of the Indians, the abolition of slavery and the subsequent treatment of blacks, a positive role of the national government in internal improvements and in setting standards for business behavior in the development of science, and positive action by the national government in the sphere of banking and the nation's monetary arrangement. In the path the nation chose, the ideology of providentialist individualism ruled events in all these areas for half a century.

Conventional treatments depict this episode as a great adventure, as "the winning of the West," "the conquering of the wilderness," or as "democratization." But these interpretations are, again, ideology in action. Within the large picture of human history, this episode seems viewed more realistically as an extraordinary victory of myopia, ignorance, and greed, as a regression into uncivilized behavior, in some cases, into barbarism.[4] The treatment of the Indians, and then of the blacks and of the Chinese and other defenseless immigrants; the despoiling of the land; the absence in the West of even rudimentary law and order and the prevalence of unpunished murder; the orgy of land speculation and land grabbing; the dominant role obviously played in the business world by speculative and predatory financial operations; the extraordinary instability of the economy and its waves of banking panics and depressions arising from application of providentialistic individualism to money-creating banks.

None of this was either inevitable or necessary. The time, after all, was not 1000 B.C. Two thousand years earlier the ancient Romans would have carried the matter off in a more orderly manner. This was an odd piece of business to conduct in the nineteenth century. The more so in a nation with the unique advantages of the United States. After all, it is a gift and not a burden to be able to take over and use an enormous tract of the world's richest land. Indeed, this *was* an opportunity unparalleled in history. John Quincy Adams was right about this. To dissipate the opportunity in land rushes and speculative fever, casual murder of Indians and one another by settlers, was not, in truth, a great human achievement. Again, the events themselves and their subsequent admiring treatments represent the ideology of providentialist individualism in action. The situation, indeed, offered the United States a unique opportunity to set quite a different kind of example for the world.

The temporary movement away from this era of licentious individualism that occurred around the turn of the century is an instructive reference point for thought about the past and the future. In its several essential characteristics, it can be viewed as an effort to move in the direction Adams had proposed half a century before. In its world view and its policy proposals, this movement rejected providentialist individualism, laissez faire, and the invisible hand. It included positive government actions for conservation of natural resources and protection of the remaining public lands, the development and application of anti-trust policy, the regulation of the railroads, the Pure Food and Drug Act, steps toward improvement of the nation's banking and monetary arrangement in the Aldrich-Vreeland Act of 1908 and establishment of the National Monetary Commission to make a comprehensive study of the subject, and pervasive actions by state governments to regulate business and set minimum standards in economic dealings.

A second and perhaps more uniquely distinguishing characteristic of this period was the effort made to de-politicize and de-ideologize areas of policy action, to apply knowledge, expertise, and a realistic, problem-solving orientation, in contrast to the polarized, unrealistic, and hate-laden ideological conflict between Social Darwinists and Populists that had dominated the scene. This element in the thought of the period was reflected in the experiments with city government by commissioners and city managers, in Theodore Roosevelt's elevation of Gifford Pinchot and the conception of professional or scientific management of the forests and natural resources, and in the establishment of independent commissions to manage particular policy areas at the national level.

Accompanying this movement to de-ideologize policy choices were a set of impressive contributions to knowledge-providing, realistic, nonideological social science and philosophy. Thorstein Veblen, John R. Commons, Wesley Mitchell, J. M. Clark, and others pointed out the unrealistic, anti-scientific, providentialist character of the prevailing version of economics. They made notable contributions—before the effort's abrupt demise in the 1940s—to create a nonideological, realistic, knowledge-providing economics. During a brief period that ended with World War I, moreover, a significant minority of American business leaders departed from the dominant business ideology of the invisible hand to build toward a realistic and responsible conception of business and its necessary relation to government.

In the same period, notable American contributions were made to a sociology which rejected Social Darwinism and sought to provide realistic understanding of the operation of societies and social organizations that could guide policies to shape a civilized society. The contributions of Lester Ward, E. A. Ross, William Graham Sumner in his late phase, and Charles H. Cooley are relevant. William James stands out as a very influential and important contributor to a parallel psychology. In philosophy, William James and John Dewey contributed to an approach oriented toward dealing effectively with reality, an orientation to which philosophers have been little inclined.

During this period, thus, there existed a rare set of forces, or ingredients, for movement by the United States toward a reasonable, civilized, knowledge-based road of development, in which responsible management of the natural habitat would be joined with like policies in other spheres. Here, again, was a road which might have been followed, followed upward, we might say, and resolutely, decade after decade. The actual outcome, however, was a resurgence of licentious individualism and know-nothingism in the 1920s, and a jumble of diverse movements in the 1930s.

The developments of recent decades are, of course, very complex and subject to no end of interpretations. The framework being applied, however, draws particular attention to the fragmentation and formalization of the social sciences, the jump of economics to a formalistic justification of providentialist individualism, the renewed ideologization of policy formation and political arrangements, the reassertion of providentialist individualism's penetration of "science," and an extraordinary resurgence of groups whose faith is providentialist individualism. The turn of the century brought economic regulation; the late 1970s saw the key to the future in deregulation.

The formalized "neoclassical" economics of recent decades contrasts with that transient period of pursuit of economic reality. The ritualized conflicts over economic policy among "Keynesians" and "monetarists," libertarians and radicals, and attackers of giant corporations and proponents of deregulation contrast with that episode of realism and pragmatism.

The enormous leaps made in recent decades in the life sciences and ecology contrast strikingly with the re-ideologized economics. But they also contrast with the rise of ideology and stylized group conflict relating to policies affecting the habitat, energy, population, the use of nuclear power, and restrictions on the automobile. Technical complexities, obscure indirect efforts of actions, and the wondrous interconnectedness of events would make a responsible, knowledge-based formation of policy for these concerns an immensely challenging organizational and intellectual problem.

The task of planning or guiding the use of new technical developments so as to preserve the habitat, the coherency of society, and the maintenance of civilized standards is, it would seem, much more demanding than that of creating new technical developments. Inventing dynamite is not so difficult as creating arrangements to assure that dynamite will be used only for beneficent purposes. Yet the organizational structures of the research laboratories of governments and corporations are models of effective organization, of the effective application of knowledge to the accomplishment of defined purposes. Applying knowledge to the broader purposes of civilized societies is very much more difficult, and the arrangements presently in effect hardly merit confidence in a favorable outcome.

The enormous challenge of the task of dealing with man's environmental crisis thus can be interpreted as arising from the disparity between two domains of beliefs, organization, and behavior. The laboratories and factories generating innovations belong to a domain of rational, knowledge-using, purposefully structured, disciplined, and task-oriented organizations. The theories, ideas, and structure of human roles in these organizations are subordinated to the successful completion of their tasks. The organizations involve a set of roles and responsibilities which provide overall guidance and procedures for the correction of failure by components to perform assigned functions. These organizations are, we know, almost alarmingly effective.

Within the framework of naturalistic thought, one would argue that the counterpart of the functional, knowledge-using structure of these organizations in achieving their narrow objectives would be a corresponding structure—a rational, knowledge-using structure—to act on behalf of society in achieving its comprehensive and complex goals and in setting rules so these innovations will not destroy the habitat or the fabric of society.

This point would not be widely accepted, of course. Here we enter the domain of providentialist ideology. No one professes that an invisible hand oversees the operations of General Motors or the Jet Propulsion Laboratory and causes these organizations to thrive no matter how their members behave—or so long as each member does what he wants to do. But, in the prevailing beliefs, it would be equally absurd to think that General Motors could get along without purposeful planning and a disciplined organizational structure and to think that the United States has any need of purposeful planning and a disciplined organizational structure. The first case is discussed in terms of functions, responsibilities, and performance; the second in terms of rights, principles, self-actualization, freedom, liberation, conservatives, liberals, radicals, and ritualized, emotion-laden group conflict.

Turn-of-the-century thinking involved efforts to de-ideologize areas of public policy. The great technical complexity and knowledge-demands of policies to protect the habitat perhaps give it a high priority for an effort to create effective organizational arrangements for the responsible application of knowledge on behalf of society. Here is a great challenge.

Closely related is the challenge of creating organizational structures that will provide the realistic knowledge needed to guide public policy. This, too, is a demanding task. Ideologized economics, with its competing sects and their competing vocabularies and ritualized policy prescriptions, illustrate the problem. Ideologized versions of evolution have figured prominently in past beliefs. Current pressures toward interpretation of evolution in terms of providentialist individualism and ideological concepts ("altruism," "aggression") illustrate the precariousness of the life sciences in a heavily ideologized world.

Further, the social sciences illustrate how academic disciplines can ingest enormous sums for "research" while generating virtually no useful knowledge, or even while destroying valid knowledge and generating false "knowledge." Competition among professionals for recognition and preferment within rules approximating laissez faire seemingly is no more certain to generate valid knowledge than a laissez faire economy is to generate valid improvement in the quality of life. Economics as presently organized is enormously efficient at generating esoteric theoretical innovations and exercises in regression analysis, but the problem-solving potentialities of its activities may be nil or negative. As is persuasively testified by the abundance of contradictory and necessarily false "knowledge" and of pseudo-science, the generation of valid knowledge is an organizational accomplishment. Here is another challenge.

This interpretation emphasizes the commonality between the present issue of environmental preservation and resource conservation and the earlier efforts of the turn of the century and the 1830s to achieve a positive, far-seeing, knowledge-based policy to use the nation's natural endowment for the long-run benefit of civilized society. New technical developments, in this interpretation, have made this task much more complex and difficult, have multiplied the demands for knowledge and analysis, have greatly increased the potential consequences of failure—have upped the ante in the game, but have not basically changed the game's nature. What is sought is still the same kind of accomplishment. The major impediment is still providentialist ideology shaped to suit the material interests and ideological posturings of various factions and groups.

This will seem to some a dissatisfactory conclusion. Perhaps it is fair to observe that since fiction can be made more satisfying than fact, the truth is not likely to be so satisfying as the various ideological stories that are its competitors. Indeed, that is the essence of the problem.

However, it can be said that this diagnosis is fundamental, that it goes to the root of the matter. Man the symbol user and symbol maker, the player of games and the inventor of games, the creator of self-satisfying roles and justificatory stories—man creates his own mind-world. But, unhappily, the joys of self-flattering mind-worlds cannot be undisturbed. Factional conflict arising from the incompatibilities of group ideologies can cause untold misery, can destroy a society.

Man must live in the physical world, must avoid destroying his habitat. To do this, whatever the providentialist delusions he sustains in other connections, he must conform to nature's rules, however offensive that discipline may seem. Nature's requirements can be met only within the framework of certain organizational structures and world views. Here is the conflict. Can man's imagination reconcile itself with nature's ways? Here is, is it not, the basic question.

Bibliography

ENVIRONMENTAL HISTORY: GENERAL WORKS

The most useful starting point for the reader interested in a further examination of historical ecology is Joseph M. Petulla, "Toward an Environmental Philosophy: In Search of a Methodology," *Environmental Review* 2 (1977); 14-43. This article surveys the development of contemporary thinking about the environment, including historical approaches, and includes an extensive bibliography. The *Chicorel Index to Environment and Ecology* (New York, 1975), vol. 16 of the *Chicorel Index Series,* also contains a bibliographical section devoted to historical aspects of ecology. For an overview of interactions between human beings and their environment, see A. S. Boughey, *Man and the Environment* (New York, 1971).

Historical demography is a basic area in the study of historical ecology. For general aspects of this subject relating to the study of environmental crisis, see A. Sauvy, *General Theory of Population* (New York, 1969), and Brian Spooner, ed., *Population Growth: Anthropological Implications* (Cambridge, 1972).

Studies of cultural regulation of hunting-gathering and early agricultural populations include L. Thompson, "A Self-Regulating System of Human Population Control," in *Transactions of the New York Academy of Sciences* 32 (1970); 262-70, and S. B. Shantzis and W. W. Behrens, "Population Control Mechanisms in a Primitive Agricultural Society," in *Toward Global Equilibrium,* ed. D. L. Meadows (Cambridge, 1973), pp. 257-88. The breakdown on population regulation in more advanced agricultural populations is considered in such works as K. Pakrasi and B. Sasmal, "Effect of

Infanticide on the Sex Ratio in an Indian Population," *Zeitschrift für Morphologie und Anthropologie* 62 (1970); 214-30, and S. N. Argarwala, *Age of Marriage in India* (Alahabad, 1962).

For the relationship of population and industrialization, see R. G. Wilkinson, *Poverty and Progress* (New York, 1973). Among many studies of the relationships between economics and fertility in industrialized societies are S. Enke, "The Economics of Having Children," *Policy Sciences* 1 (1970); 6-30, and A. Sweezy, "The Economic Explanation of Fertility Changes in the U.S.," *Population Studies* 25, no. 2 (1971); 255-67.

Relationships among economic and environmental factors and future population movements are examined in such works as D. H. Meadows, et al., *The Limits of Growth,* 2nd ed. (New York, 1975), and A. S. Boughey, *Strategy for Survival* (Menlo Park, Cal., 1976).

Climatic factors are also basic elements in environmental history. Two recent works surveying this field are Reid A. Bryson, *Climates of Hunger: Mankind and the World's Changing Weather* (Madison, Wis., 1977), and S. H. Schneider, *The Genesis Strategy* (New York, 1976).

ECOLOGICAL CRISES IN PREHISTORY

A basic work dealing with man's early ecological setting is Karl W. Butzer, *Environment and Archaeology* (Chicago, 1964). For an approach to functional relationships between man and his environment, see Marvin Harris, *Culture, People, Nature: An Introduction to General Anthropology,* 2nd ed. (New York, 1975), and *Cannibals and Kings, The Origins of Culture* (New York, 1977), by the same author. On the culture of the Indus Valley, see Sir Mortimer Wheeler, *The Indus Civilization* (Cambridge, 1968). On the development of sedentism in the Near East, see Lewis R. Binford, "Post Pleistocene Adaptations," in *New Perspectives in Archaeology,* ed. Sally R. Binford and Lewis R. Binford (Chicago, 1968). Pleistocene animal extinction in the New World is discussed in Paul S. Martin, "The Discovery of America," *Science* 179 (1973); 969-74. On conditions in Greenland, see H. H. Lamb, *The Changing Climate* (London, 1966), Erik Erngaard, *Greenland, Then and Now* (Copenhagen, 1972), and Gwyn Jones, *A History of the Vikings* (New York, 1968). For the Pueblo culture, see Paul S. Martin and Fred Plog, *The Archaeology of Arizona: A Study of the Southwest Region* (Garden City, N.Y., 1973). Concerning the Aztecs, see

Michael Harner, "The Enigma of Aztec Sacrifice," *Natural History* 86, no. 4 (1977); 46-51.

ECOLOGICAL CRISES IN CLASSICAL ANTIQUITY

A number of valuable works are available that give a general introduction to the ecology of the Greek and Roman world. E. C. Semple, *The Geography of the Mediterranean Region* (New York, 1931); M. Cary, *The Geographic Background of Greek and Roman History* (Oxford, 1949); and M. Grant, *The Ancient Mediterranean* (New York, 1969), are fine, detailed studies. J. Donald Hughes in his *Ecology in Ancient Civilizations* (Albuquerque, 1975), presents a general survey of ancient environmental history with an emphasis on the interactions of the attitudes of ancient peoples with their environments. Important works stressing the economic and social aspects of ancient history are M. Rostovtzeff, *The Social and Economic History of the Hellenistic World,* 3 vols. (Oxford, 1941); *The Social and Economic History of the Roman Empire,* 2nd ed., 2 vols. (Oxford, 1957); F. M. Heichelheim, *An Ancient Economic History,* 3 vols. (Leiden, 1958-70); and Jean-Philippe Levy, *The Economic Life of the Ancient World* (Chicago, 1964).

For those with an interest in what many historians regard as specific examples of what are termed today "ecological crises," the following periods and works are recommended. John Chadwick's *The Mycenaean World* (Cambridge, 1976), makes a careful study of Mycenaean civilization with much attention paid to environmental factors; of special interest are his views concerning the effects of the volcanic destruction of the island of Thera on the decline of Minoan civilization. The causes of Greek colonization in the eighth century B.C. are related by many scholars to the effects of overpopulation on a limited ecosystem; see A. Gwynn, "The Character of Greek Colonization," *Journal of Hellenic Studies* 38 (1918); 88-123, J. Hasebroek, *Trade and Politics in Ancient Greece* (London, 1933), and J. L. Angel, "Ecology and Population in the Eastern Mediterranean," *World Archaeology* 4 (1972); 88-105.

With reference to Roman history, many historians have seen the decline of the small farmer in the last century and a half of the Roman Republic as leading to the eventual collapse of the Republic; see C. Yeo, "The Development of the Roman Plantation and Marketing of Farm Products," *Finanzarchiv* 13 (1951-52); 321-42, P. A. Brunt, "The Army and the Land in the Roman Revolution,"

Journal of Roman Studies 52 (1962); 69-86, and A. H. Bernstein, *Tiberius Sempronius Gracchus: Tradition and Apostasy* (Ithaca, 1978). Arnold Toynbee, *Hannibal's Legacy,* 2 vols. (Oxford, 1965), states that much of this decline was due to the devastations of Hannibal's invasion of Italy. The fall of the Roman Empire also is seen as having ecological elements; this is discussed in V. G. Simkhovitch, "Rome's Fall Reconsidered," *Political Science Quarterly* 31 (1916); 201-43, E. Huntington, "Climate Change and Agricultural Exhaustion as Elements in the Fall of Rome," *Quarterly Journal of Economics* 31 (1917); 173-208, and A. E. R. Boak, *Manpower Shortage and the Fall of the Roman Empire in the West* (Ann Arbor, 1955).

ECOLOGICAL CRISIS IN ANCIENT CHINA

There are no works dealing specifically with this topic. Several books, however, can be consulted for a good general background to the political, cultural, and economic trends of the time. These include C. Y. Hsu, *Ancient China in Transition* (Stanford, Cal., 1965); R. L. Walker, *The Multi-State System of Ancient China* (Hamden, Conn., 1953); T. K. Cheng, *Archaeology in China,* vol. 3: *Chou China* (Cambridge, 1963); and K. C. Chang, *The Archaeology of Ancient China,* 3rd ed. (New Haven, 1977).

Most of our information about the period is found in three major historical sources, the *Ch'un Ch'iu,* the *Tso Chuan,* and Ssu-ma Ch'ien's *Shih Chi.* The standard translations of these texts are J. Legge, *The Ch'un Ts'ew with the Tso Chuen,* vol. 5 of *The Chinese Classics,* 5 vols. (Hong Kong, 1960), and E. Chavannes, *Les mémoires historiques de Se-ma Ts'ien,* 5 vols. (Paris, 1895-1905). An important philosophical source dealing extensively with ecology-related problems has been translated by J. J. L. Duyvendak as *The Book of Lord Shang* (Chicago, 1963).

ENVIRONMENTAL HISTORY OF THE EUROPEAN MIDDLE AGES

General and regional studies on the early medieval period are numerous. On the climate of the time, see W. Dansgaard, "One Thousand Centuries of Climatic Record from Camp Century on the Greenland Ice Sheet," *Science* 166 (1969); 377-81. For early Medieval population, see J. C. Russell, *Late Ancient and Medieval*

Population (Philadelphia, 1958), and especially "The Earlier Medieval Plague in the British Isles," *Viator* 7 (1976), as well as J. LeGoff, "La Peste dans le Haut Moyen-age," *Annales: E.S.C.* 24 (1933), N. H. Baynes, "The Decline of Roman Power in Western Europe. Some Modern Explanations," *Journal of Roman Studies* 33 (1933), C. Curtois, *Les Vandales de l'Afrique* (Paris, 1954), pp. 97-104, and E. W. Bovill, *The Golden Trade of the Moors,* 2nd ed. (Oxford, 1970), pp. 28-57. For agricultural decline in the western Mediterranean during the late ancient period, see R. W. Bulliet, *The Camel and the Wheel* (Cambridge, Mass., 1975), A. Dupont, *Les cités de la Narbonnaise première depuis les invasions germaniques jusqu'à l'apparition du consulat* (Nimes, 1942), pp. 1-83, P. Wolff, *Histoire du Languedoc* (Toulouse, 1967), pp. 99-110, and F. Cheyette, "The Origins of European Villages and the First European Expansion," *Journal of Economic History* 37 (1977).

For the eastern Mediterranean, see E. Ashtor, *A Social and Economic History of the Near East in Medieval Times* (Berkeley, 1976), pp. 1-134. For the Black Sea and Aegean area, R. Janin, *Constantinople byzantine: dévelopment urbain et répetoire topographique* (Paris, 1950), and H. Ahrweiler, *Byzance et la mer* (Paris, 1966), pp. 175-225, contain much information on dockyards and timber resources. See also A. R. Lewis, "Mediterranean Maritime Commerce A.D. 300-1100. Shipping and Trade," *La Navigazione Mediterranea nell' alto Medioevo,* vol. 25 in *Settimani di Studi sull' alto medioevo* (Spoleto, 1978). For the maritime area located on the Atlantic and Mediterranean sides of the Straits of Gibraltar, see J. Devisse, "Routes de commerce et échanges en Afrique occidentale en relation avec la Mediterranée," *Revue d'histoire économique et sociale* 50 (1971), A. R. Lewis, "Northern European Sea-power and the Straits of Gilbraltar, 1031-1350," in *Order and Innovation in the Middle Ages,* ed. Jordan, McNab, and Ruiz (Princeton, 1976), pp. 152-63, J. N. Hillgarth, *The Problem of a Catalan Maritime Empire,* in the *English Historical Review,* Supplement no. 8 (1975), and C. Verlinden, "Les Genois dans la marine portugaise avant 1385," *Studia Historia Gandensis* 41 (Ghent, 1966).

For the early development of shipping in northern Europe, see A. R. Lewis, *The Northern Seas* (Princeton, 1958), and O. Crumlin Pederson, "The Vikings and the Hanseatic Merchants, 900-1450," in *A History of Seafaring* (London, 1976). For North Sea commerce during the Middle Ages, see A. Bridbury, *England and the Salt Trade in the Later Middle Ages* (London, 1955), M. K. James, *Studies in the Medieval Wine Trade* (London, 1971), D. Burwash,

English Merchant Shipping, 1460-1540 (Toronto, 1969), and R. W. Unger, "The Netherlands' Herring Fishery in the Late Middle Ages," *Viator* 9 (1978); 335-56.

Concerning the economic expansion of the twelfth and thirteenth centuries, a recent work intended for educated laymen is Jean Gimpel, *The Medieval Machine: The Industrial Revolution of the Middle Ages* (New York, 1976), but one should not take his concluding chapters too seriously. More scholarly, but also intended for a popular audience is R. de Molen, ed. *One Thousand Years: Western Europe in the Middle Ages*, (Boston, 1974), which contains essays by such scholars as D. Herlihy, D. Nicholas, D. Queller, et al., and the first volume of C. Cipolla, ed., *Fontana Economic History of Europe*, (London, 1972), especially the contribution by Lynn White Jr., "The Expansion of Technology, 500-1500." White has done more than any other scholar to deepen our knowledge of medieval technology in such works as *Medieval Technology and Social Change* (Oxford, 1962), "What Accelerated Technological Progress in the Western Middle Ages," in *Scientific Change,* ed. A. C. Crombie (New York, 1963), and "Cultural Climates and Technological Advance in the Middle Ages," *Viator* 2 (1971). Useful articles are R. de Roover, "The Commercial Revolution of the Thirteenth Century," in *Enterprise and Secular Change,* ed. F. Lane and J. Riemersma (1953), and E. M. Carus-Wilson, "An Industrial Revolution of the 13th Century," in Carus-Wilson, *Essays in Economic History,* vol. I (London, 1954).

The most comprehensive and stimulating short statement of the contraction of the fourteenth century is A. R. Lewis, "The Closing of the Medieval Frontier," *Speculum* 33 (1958). The best short economic histories of the period are R. S. Lopez, *The Commercial Revolution of the Middle Ages, 950-1350* (Englewood Cliffs, N.J., 1970), H. Miskimin, *The Economy of Early Renaissance Europe 1300-1460* (Englewood Cliffs, N.J., 1969), and C. Cipolla, *Before the Industrial Revolution: European Society and Economy, 1000-1700* (New York, 1976). The careful reader will note that Cipolla's views differ considerably from those of Lopez and Miskimin. Anyone interested in the agrarian basis of the medieval economy should read G. Duby, *Rural Economy, and Country Life in the Medieval West,* trans. C. Postan (Columbia, S.C., 1968). For the role of the landlord in the medieval economy, see R. Witt, "The Landlord and the Economic Revival of the Middle Ages in Northern Europe, 1000-1250," *American Historical Review* 76 (1971), and B. Lyon, "Medieval Real Estate Developments and Freedom," *American*

Historical Review 63 (1957). D. Herlihy shows how general economic movements affected the life of a particular community in *Medieval and Renaissance Pistoia: The Social History of an Italian Town, 1200-1430* (New Haven, 1967). A recent book describing how merchants reacted to the crisis is B. Kedar, *Merchants in Crisis: Genoese and Venetian Men of Affairs and the Fourteenth Century Depression* (New Haven, 1976). For the cultural anxiety of the period, see R. Kieckhefer, *European Witch Trials: Their Foundations in Popular and Learned Culture, 1300-1500* (London, 1976).

Examples of medieval European historical and theological comment upon Judeo-Christian attitudes toward the environment may be found in Frederick Edler, *Crisis in Eden: A Religious Study of Man and Environment* (Nashville, 1970); C.F.D. Moule, *Man and Nature in the New Testament* (Philadelphia, 1967); George H. Williams, *Wilderness and Paradise in Christian Thought* (New York, 1962); Conrad Bonifazi, *A Theology of Things* (Philadelphia, 1967); *Christians and the Good Earth: Addresses and Discussions at the Third National Conference of the Faith-Man-Nature Group*, F/M/N Papers, no. 1 (Warrenton, 1967); Michael Hamilton, ed., *The Little Planet*, intro. Edmund S. Muskie (New York, 1970); A. M. Klaus Müller and Wolfhart Pannenberg, *Erwägungen zu einer Theologie der Natur* (Gütersloh, 1970). A brief survey of medieval demography with bibliography is David Herlihy, "Economic Conditions and Demographic Change," pp. 1-43, in *One Thousand Years: Western Europe in the Middle Ages*, ed. Richard L. DeMolen (Boston, 1974). Studies dealing with the new spirit of the twelfth century are Zullio Gregory, *Anima Mundi: La filosofia di Guglielmo di Conches e la Scuola di Chartres* (Florence, 1955); M. D. Chenu, *Nature, Man, and Society in the Twelfth Century. Essays on New Theological Perspectives in the Latin West*, preface by Etienne Gilson, ed. and trans. Jerome Taylor and Lester K. Little (Chicago, 1968).

ECOLOGICAL HISTORY OF POST-MEDIEVAL EUROPE

Perhaps because of its great and immediate dependence upon natural forces, pre-industrial Europe has attracted considerable attention from ecological historians. General works on the physical environment include the useful surveys of C. T. Smith, *An Historical Geography of Western Europe Before 1800* (New York, 1967), and Hugh D. Clout, ed., *Themes in the Historical Geography of*

France (London, 1977); seminal among studies of climate is Emmanuel LeRoy Ladurie, *Times of Feast, Times of Famine: A History of Climate Since the Year 1000* (Garden City, 1971), which examines both shifts in climatological conditions and the evidence used to determine them. The greatest use of the ecological approach for this (and possibly any) period is made by Fernand Braudel, most notably in *The Mediterranean in the Age of Philip II* (New York, 1972, 1973), and also in *Capitalism and Material Life, 1400-1800* (New York, 1973). Braudel is a member of the *Annales* School, so called because of its association with the journal *Annales: économies, sociétés, civilisations,* founded in 1929 by Marc Bloch and Lucien Febvre, which has published pioneering articles on social, economic, and ecological history and continues to do so. Written under Braudel's influence, though less concerned with physical environment, is Immanuel Wallerstein, *The Modern World System: Capitalist Agriculture and the Origins of the European World Economy in the Sixteenth Century* (New York, 1976). Much scholarship on the pre-industrial period has been focused on the political and social impact of dearth. The material conditions for the period are sketched by Carlo Cipolla in *Before the Industrial Revolution: European Society and Economy 1000-1700* (New York, 1976). George Rudé in *The Crowd in History, 1730-1848* (New York, 1964), and Richard Cobb in *The Police and the People: French Popular Protest, 1789-1820* (London, 1970), discuss popular responses to food shortages; Steven Kaplan in *Bread, Politics, and Political Economy in the Reign of Louis XV* (The Hague, 1976), takes more the view "from above" when analyzing how pre-industrial France was provisioned and the political forces acting on the administration of food policy under the Old Regime. On changing attitudes toward nature and man's ability to control his environment, see Clarence J. Glacken, *Traces on the Rhodian Shore: Nature and Culture in Western Thought from Ancient Times to the End of the Eighteenth Century* (Berkeley, 1967), and Paolo Rossi, *Philosophy, Technology, and the Arts in the Early Modern Era* (New York, 1970).

Some of the ecological implications of the industrial period are dealt with in J. D. Chambers and G. E. Mingay, *The Agricultural Revolution, 1750-1880* (New York, 1966), and E. A. Wrigley, "The Supply of Raw Materials in the Industrial Revolution," *Economic History Review* 15 (1962); 1-16. Demographic movements are considered in two collections of articles, D. V. Glass and D. E. V. Eversley, ed., *Population in History: Essays in Historical Demography* (Chicago, 1965), and Michael Drake, ed., *Population in*

Industrialization (London, 1969). Asa Briggs discusses urbanization in the nineteenth century in *Victorian Cities* (New York, 1963). Louis Chevalier brings together demographic, urban, medical, and literary history in his unique *Laboring Classes and Dangerous Classes in Paris During the First Half of the Nineteenth Century* (New York, 1973). Agrarian developments and their social impact are examined by C. Woodham Smith, *The Great Hunger* (New York, 1962), and Eric Hobsbawn and George Rudé, *Captain Swing: A Social History of the Great Agricultural Uprising of 1830* (New York, 1975).

Cities in the industrial era have also generated an extensive body of literature. A general survey of urban ecology will be found in Anthony M. Davis and Thomas F. Glick, "Urban Ecosystems and Urban Biogeography," in press. For an example of a medical-geographical study sensitive to the natural, but not man-made, environmental features of urban epidemiology, see A. A. Brownlea, "An Urban Ecology of Infectious Disease: City of Greater Wollongong-Shellharbour," *Australian Geographer* 10 (1967); 169-87. On urban climatology generally, see James T. Peterson, *The Climate of Cities: A Survey of Recent Literature* (Raleigh, N. C., 1969). For the biometeorological approach, see J. K. Page, "The Effect of Town Planning and Architectural Design and Construction on the Microclimatic Environment of Man," in *Medical Biometeorology*, ed. S. W. Tromp (Amsterdam, 1963), pp. 655-70. W. H. Terjung, "The Energy Balance Climatology of a City-Man System," *Annals of the Association of American Geographers* 60 (1970); 466-92, a recent study of biotic repercussions of energy exchanges of storage within the city, deals only with man, when it seems clear that the heat-retention capability of urban structures must have greater measurable effect on other forms of life, microbes in particular. On rats in cities, see John B. Calhoun, *The Ecology and Sociology of the Norway Rat* (Bethesda, 1963), R. A. Davis, "Occurrence of the Black Rat in Sewers in Britain," *Nature* 175 (1955); 641, and Henry Mayhew, *London Labour and the London Poor*, 4 vols. (New York, 1968), II; 431-33. On urban drainage in both London and the United States, see Sylvia Thrupp, *The Merchant Class of Medieval London* (Chicago, 1948), pp. 137-38, Stuart Galishoff, "Drainage, Disease, Comfort, and Class: A History of Newark's Sewers," *Societas* 6 (1976); 121-38, and Mark J. Tierno, "The Search for Pure Water in Pittsburgh: The Urban Response to Water Pollution, 1893-1914," *Western Pennsylvania Historical Magazine* 60 (1977); 23-36.

THE ENVIRONMENT IN THE UNITED STATES

For the reader interested in a full treatment of the extensive literature on American concern with the environment, Roderick Nash's *The American Environment: Readings in the History of Conservation* (Reading, Mass., 1976), provides an excellent, analytical introduction. European ideas brought to the Americas by colonists in the seventeenth and eighteenth centuries quickly changed when they confronted the American wilderness, a shift demonstrated by Roderick Nash in *Wilderness and the American Mind* (New Haven, 1967), and by Russel B. Nye in "The American View of Nature," in his *This Almost Chosen People: Essays in the History of American Ideas* (East Lansing, Mich., 1966). Hans Huth, *Nature and the Americans* (Berkeley, 1957), provides a useful examination of the further change in the American view through the nineteenth and twentieth centuries.

The growth of conservationism has attracted considerable attention. Huth's *Nature and the Americans* comes closest to a synthetic view of the development of this idea. Most of this literature, however, still focuses on the development of specific conservation groups. Two primary documents critical to an understanding of the general growth of the idea of environmental limits in the United States are George P. Marsh, *The Earth as Modified by Human Action* (New York, 1874), and Frederick Jackson Turner, *The Frontier in American History* (New York, 1920). Each of these studies was an important call for Americans to reevaluate their relationships with and their uses of nature. A good starting point for the history of the individual movements that grew out of concern for the problem of conservation is Henry Clepper, ed. *Origins of American Conservation* (New York, 1966). This work is a series of essays on the development of efforts to regulate the uses of forests, fisheries, and wildlife.

The development of political conservationism that accompanied the emergence of Progressivism is another major area of interest. One of the most enlightening documents giving the Progressive conservationist point of view is Gifford Pinchot's autobiographical *The Fight for Conservation* (Garden City, N.J., 1910). Pinchot introduced the idea that conservation, as it developed in the late nineteenth century, was a movement aimed at the protection of the public welfare. A document supporting Pinchot and also derived from the movement is Charles R. Van Hise, *The Conservation of Natural Resources* (New York, 1910). An important modern criticism of this view is Samuel P. Hays, *Conservation and the Gospel of Efficiency: The Progressive Conservation Movement, 1890-1920* (Cambridge, Mass., 1959). Hays argues that conservation was as much a scientific movement designed to bring about expert, professional development of resources so that they could be better utilized as one for the public's well-being. Elmo R. Richardson chronicles the triumph of modern political conservationism in *The Politics of Conservation: Crusades and Controversies, 1897-1913* (Berkeley, 1962). Indicating the lack of consensus among the conservationists, especially over the question of the state's role in the matter of regulation, the Ballinger-Pinchot affair is a key issue, and James L. Penick indicates its dimensions in *Progressive Politics and Conservation: The Ballinger-Pinchot Affair* (Chicago, 1968). Penick offers an excellent insight into other problems of the movement in "The Progressives and the Environment: Three Themes from the First Conservation Movement," in *The Progressive Era*, ed. Lewis L. Gould (Syracuse, N.Y., 1974).

Important observations on the history of political conservationism after the Progressive Era are Donald Swain's *Federal Conservation Policy, 1921-1933* (Berkeley, 1963), and Elmo R. Richardson, *Dams, Parks and Politics: Resource Development and Preservation in the Truman-Eisenhower Era* (Lexington, Ky., 1973).

Two important historiographical studies of American conservation may be found in Gordon B. Dodds, "The Historiography of American Conservation: Past and Prospects," *Pacific Northwest Quarterly* 56 (1965); 75-81, and Lawrence Rakestraw, "Conservation Historiography: An Assessment," *Pacific Historical Review* 41 (1972); 271-88.

ENVIRONMENTAL HISTORY AND ECONOMIC THEORY

For an account of the development of the conception of progress in Western thought, see J. B. Bury, *The Idea of Progress* (New York, 1932). A popular discussion of the intellectual tides from which individualistic economics emerged is given in J. Bronowski and Bruce Mazlish, *The Western Intellectual Tradition* (New York, 1975). An excellent presentation of modern Darwinian thought and criticism of providentialism is given in Garrett Hardin, *Nature and Man's Fate* (New York, 1959). That in the nineteenth-century United States the doctrine of vox populi comprised a kind of providentialism is argued in Gordon S. Wood, "The Democratization of Mind in the American Revolution," in *The Moral Foundations of the American Republic,* ed. Robert H. Horwitz (Charlottesville, 1977).

A brief and lively treatment of the development of economics that brings out the shortcomings of the invisible hand doctrine is Guy Routh, *The Origin of Economic Ideas* (New York, 1975). Major criticisms of the unrealism and the providentialist nature of conventional economics and Marxist economics from turn-of-the-century thought are Thorstein Veblen, "Why Is Economics Not an Evolutionary Science," "The Preconceptions of the Classical Economists," and "The Socialist Economics of Karl Marx," reprinted in Max Lerner, ed., *The Portable Veblen* (New York, 1948). The best treatment of American "institutionalist economists" is Allan G. Gruchy, *Modern Economic Thought: The American Contribution* (New York, 1967). The environmental implications of economic growth are discussed and extensive references provided in Herman E. Daly, *Steady-State Economics* (San Francisco, 1977), chaps. 1, 2. A useful collection of readings on this subject is Daly, ed., *Toward A Steady-State Economy* (San Francisco, 1973). On responsible relations between business and government in an early period, see Alfred L. Thimm, *Business Ideologies in the Reform-Progressive Era, 1880-1914* (University, Ala., 1976), pp. 198-99.

Notes

CHAPTER 2: HOFFMAN

1. Barbara G. Beddall, "Letter to the Editor," *Science* 180 (1973); 905.
2. Michael Harner, "The Enigma of Aztec Sacrifice," *Natural History* 86, no. 4 (1977); 49.
3. *Ibid.*, p. 51.
4. Mark Cohen, *The Food Crisis in Prehistory* (New Haven, 1977), p. 285.

CHAPTER 3: HUGHES

1. Plutarch, *Alexander* 64.2.
2. Theocritus 4.43, quoted in W. K. C. Guthrie, *The Greeks and Their Gods* (Boston, 1954), p. 38.
3. Homeric *Hymn to Aphrodite* 5.3-5.
4. Euripides, *Alcestis* 578 ff.
5. Homeric *Hymn to Pan* 19.5-11.
6. Catullus 34.9 ff.
7. Sophocles, *Electra* 563-72.
8. Guthrie, p. 100.
9. Aeschylus, *Agamemnon* 135-43.
10. Xenophon, *Cynegeticus* 5.14. Another survival from hunting and gathering societies may be seen in the offerings of fruit and meal-cakes left by Greek rhizotomists to "pay" for certain herbs (Theophrastus, *Historia Plantarum* 9.8.7). American Indian medicine men and women had similar rituals.
11. Kenneth Clark, "Animals and Men: Love, Admiration, and Outright War," *Smithsonian,* 8 (September 1977); 55.
12. Pliny, *Natural History* 13.3.
13. Pausanias 8.54.5.
14. Homeric *Hymn to Delian Apollo* 3.22-24.
15. Homeric *Hymn to Earth the Mother of All* 30.1-4.
16. Guthrie, p. 58.
17. John Rodman, "The Other Side of Ecology in Ancient Greece: Comments on Hughes," *Inquiry,* 19 (Spring 1976); 108-12.

18. Empedocles, fragment 8.
19. Lucretius, *De Rerum Natura* 2.75-79.
20. Diogenes Laertius, *Life of Empedocles* 12.
21. Iamblichus, *Life of Pythagoras* 186.
22. Empedocles, fragment 137.
23. Diogenes Laertius, *Life of Pythagoras* 8.4.
24. Empedocles, fragment 117.
25. Empedocles, fragment 17.
26. Empedocles, fragments 8-9, translated in Philip Wheelwright, *The Presocratics* (New York, 1966), p. 127.
27. Anaxagoras, fragment 6.
28. Here I have ignored the question of authorship, simply postulating my "Hippocrates" as the author of this one work.
29. These quotations are from George Sessions, "Spinoza and Jeffers: An Environmental Perspective," *Inquiry*, 20 (1977), 481-528.
30. Aristotle, *Metaphysics* 12.10.2 (107a17-20).
31. George Sarton, *A History of Science: Ancient Science Through the Golden Age of Greece* (Cambridge, Mass., 1952), p. 565; Friedrich S. Bodenheimer, "Aristotle, the Father of Animal Ecology," *Homenaje a Millas-Valliciosa* (Barcelona, 1954), pp. 165-81.
32. Aristotle, *Historia Animalium* 9.1 (609b19-25).
33. *Ibid.* (610a34-35).
34. *Ibid.* 6.36 (580b10-29).
35. *Ibid.* 5.15 (547b15-32).
36. *Ibid.* 8.1 (588a13-b17); see also *De Partibus Animalium* 4.5 (681a12 ff).
37. Anthony Preus, *Science and Philosophy in Aristotle's Biological Works* (Hildesheim, 1975), p. 217.
38. *Ibid.*, Aristotle, *Politics* 1.5 (1254b18-19), 1.8 (1256b15-26).
39. Preus attributes to "some modern scientists" belief in a "democratic" theory of ecology "which supposes that all living things have an intrinsic value which is absolute, that the value, merit, or worth of any living thing is to be regarded as intrinsically equal to that of any other; living things are not arranged in a scale of value" (p. 324, n. 48). Neither the "aristocratic" or "democratic" theory is scientific; they are philosophical models which might, perhaps, serve as guides for human technology. But the pure structure of the democratic model is more similar to the reticulum disclosed by scientific ecology and seems, therefore, better to reflect reality.
40. Theophrastus, *Metaphysics* 9.32-34, quoted in Clarence J. Glacken, *Traces on the Rhodian Shore* (Berkeley, 1967), p. 51. I am indebted to Glacken for his exegesis of Theophrastus.
41. Vitruvius, *De Architectura* 8.6.11; see also 8.3.5, 8.4.1-2, 8.6.10-13.
42. Strabo, *Geography* 3.2.8 (c. 147).
43. Xenophon, *Oeconomicus* 2.10-15. See Columella, *De Re Rustica* 1. pref. 1-3.
44. Horace, *Carmina* 3.1.36-37.
45. *Ibid.* 3.29.12.
46. Seneca, *Epistulae Morales* 90.7-13.
47. Martial 12.57.4-6.
48. Plutarch, *Moralia* 962C-D.
49. *Ibid.* 996F.
50. *Ibid.* 999A, referring to Hesiod, *Works and Days*, 277-79.
51. But Plutarch could be conventional; see his *Life of Pericles*, 1. For a review of recent writings on animal rights, see John Rodman, "The Liberation of Nature?" *Inquiry*, 20 (Spring 1977); 83, 131.

CHAPTER 4: BILSKY

1. J. Legge, *The Works of Mencius*, 2 of *The Chinese Classics*, 5 vols. (Hong Kong, 1960), p. 148.
2. See Legge, *Mencius*, pp. 132, 173, 217, 242; H. H. Dubs, *The Works of Hsüntze* (London, 1928), p. 180.
3. United Nations, Population Division, "History of Population Theories," in *Population Theory and Policy*, ed. J. J. Spengler and Duncan, O.D. (Glencoe, Ill., 1956), p. 6.
4. A. Sauvy, *General Theory of Population* (New York, 1969), p. 52.
5. B. Watson, *Records of the Grand Historian of China* (2 vols.; New York, 1961), II, 71.
6. J. I. Crump, Jr., *Chan-kuo Ts'e* (Oxford, 1970), pp. 199-200.

CHAPTER 5: LEWIS

1. We know little about the earlier salt trade. However, for a later period, see H. Noiret, *Domination vénetienne en Crete;* Documents (1892) pp. 65-68, 476-83.
2. On Porphyrio, one of these whales, see Procopius, *Anecdola* 15; and *Gothic Wars* III, 29. See some comments on these whales in W. G. Holmes, *The Age of Justinian and Theodora II* (London, 1912), pp. 368, 643.
3. *Notitia Dignitatum Occid*, ed. Seekt, XLII, 4 and 7, p. 215. Also A. R. Lewis, *Naval Power and Trade in the Mediterranean, A.D. 500-1100* (Princeton, 1951) pp. 43-44.
4. *The Bayeux Tapestry*, ed. Maclagan, (rev. ed.; Harmondsworth, 1949); and M. Mollat, "Les Marines et la guerre dans le nord et l'ouest de l' Europe," *Settimani di Studi del Centro Italiano*, 15 (Spoleto, 1968). See also P. Riant, *Expeditions et pélerinages des Scandinaves en Terre Sainte* (Paris, 1865) pp. 1-103.
5. See *De Expugnatione Lyxbonense*, ed. C. David (New York, 1936); and T. A. Archer, *The Crusade of Richard I* (London, 1912).
6. Not enough has been made of the role of England's Forest Laws in preserving ship timber reserves for royal and other fleets. On these fleets, see F. W. Brooks, *The English Naval Forces, 1199-1272* (Manchester, 1932; 1962).
7. See G. Jones, *The North Atlantic Saga* (London, 1964) for the best account of these voyages.
8. P. G. Foote and D. N. Wilson, *The Viking Achievement*, p. 202, date the development of Lofoten cod fisheries from only the twelfth century. On ship building here, see *ibid.*, pp. 250-51; and Brøgger and Shetelig, *The Viking Ships*, (2nd ed.; Oslo, 1971), pp. 186-235.
9. For the development of new and superior types of northern ships see A. McKee, "The Influence of British Naval Strategy on Ship Design," in *A History of Seafaring*, pp. 226-30, and W. A. Baker, "Fishing under Sail in the North Atlantic," in the *Atlantic World of Robert G. Albion*, pp. 42-43.

CHAPTER 6: BOWLUS

1. Postan's review of Duby, *Rural Economy*, in *Economic History Review*, series 2, 16 (1963); 197: "The present reviewer has been especially gratified to read the passages in this book wherein the depression of the 14th century is represented as the consequence, perhaps even the nemesis, of the inordinate expansion of the preceding epoch."

2. The most important opponent of Postan and Lopez is C. Cipolla. See especially his "Economic Depression of the Renaissance?" *Economic History Review,* series 2, 17 (1964); 519-29. Cipolla's quarrel, however, seems to be with the word "depression," for he freely admits in *Before the Industrial Revolution: European Society and Economy, 1000-1700* (New York, 1976), pp. 198-204, that the fourteenth and fifteenth centuries were a difficult period in European history. He argues that the wars and plagues of these centuries reduced population so that although the gross product was less than in the preceding period, per capita productivity increased.

CHAPTER 7: HERLIHY

1. It should be noted, however, that even primitive and poorly productive economies are capable of inflicting severe ecological damage. One of the most dramatic examples of this is the deforestation, overgrazing, erosion, and soil exhaustion of Mediterranean lands during the period of the Roman empire. See the now classical statement by Vladimir G. Simkhovitch, *Toward the Understanding of Jesus and Two Additional Historical Studies: Rome's Fall Reconsidered and Hay in History* (New York, 1947). On erosion as a factor in the decline of civilizations, see Vernon G. Carter and Tom Dale, *Topsoil and Civilization,* rev. ed. (Norman, Okla., 1974), especially pp. 55-155.
2. "The Historical Roots of Our Ecologic Crisis," *Science* 155 (1967); 1203-07.
3. Genesis 1.28, *The Holy Bible* (New York, 1901).
4. *Ibid.,* 3.17-19.
5. Saint Augustine, *Against Julian,* trans. Matthew A. Schumacher, C. S. C., *The Fathers of the Church, A New Translation* (New York, 1977), p. 21.
6. *Tertulliani Opera,* Pars II, *Opera monastica* (Corpus Christianorum, Series Latina, 2; Turnholt, 1954), p. 827.
7. *Ibid.*
8. Ad Demetrianum, *S. Thasci Caecili Cypriani Opera omnia* (Corpus Scriptorum Ecclesiasticorum Latinorum, 3, 1; Vienna, 1868), pp. 352-53.
9. See, for example, his sermon in *Opera omnia,* V (Paris, 1837), col. 628.
10. Saint Augustine, *Treatises on Marriage and Other Subjects, Fathers of the Church, A New Translation* (New York, 1955), pp. 21-34.
11. *Ibid.,* p. 159, from the tract *Contra Jovinianum.*
12. *Ibid.,* p. 166.
13. Sermo 250. *Opera omnia,* V (Paris, 1837), 1506.
14. Lucretius, *On the Nature of the Universe (De rerum natura),* trans. James H. Mantinband (New York, 1965), p. 67, lines 1157-74.
15. Contra Jovinianum, *Patrologia latina,* ed. J. P. Migne, XXIII (Paris, 1855), col. 211ff.
16. Cited in Simkhovitch, *Understanding,* p. 126.
17. George H. Williams, *Wilderness and Paradise in Christian Thought* (New York, 1962), examines at length the somewhat paradoxical attitudes toward wilderness and paradise in Biblica and Christian thought.
18. *Martini episcopi bracarensis Opera omnia,* ed. C. W. Barlow (New Haven, 1950), cap. 16.
19. *Beowulf,* trans. Burton Raffel (New York, 1963), lines 3062-65.
20. Quoted from M. D. Chenu, *Man and Society in the Twelfth Century* (Chicago, 1968), p. 19.
21. *Ibid.,* p. 41.
22. *The Complaint of Nature,* trans. Douglas M. Moffat, Yale Studies in English, no. 36 (New York, 1908).

23. Guillaume de Lorris and Jean de Meun, *The Romance of the Rose*, trans. Charles Dahlberg (Princeton, 1971), p. 324, line 19701.
24. This is the estimate (two million in ca. 1300) of Enrico Fiumi. For further discussion, see David Herlihy, *Medieval and Renaissance Pistoia. The Social History of an Italian Town, 1200-1430* (New Haven, 1967), p. 114.
25. For a recent, critical discussion of this Malthusian thesis, see Robert Brenner, "Agrarian Class Structure and Economic Development in Pre-Industrial Europe," *Past and Present* 70 (1976); 30-75.
26. In Italy, for example, the religious movement known as the Grand Company of the Whites, which swept through many northern cities in 1399, was based in large part upon the expectation that the end of the world was approaching. See Herlihy, *Pistoia*, pp. 250ff.
27. *The Goliard Poets. Medieval Latin Songs and Satires*, ed. George F. Whicher (New York, 1949), p. 198.
28. Cited in David Herlihy, *Medieval Culture and Society* (New York, 1968), p. 233.
29. "Selve d'Amore. Stanze," *Opere*, ed. A. Simioni, 2 vols. (Bari, 1913-14), I; 243-86.
30. An English translation of the Latin letter to Francesco Dionigi de'Roberti, which describes the ascent, is available in *The Renaissance Philosophy of Man*, ed. Ernst Carrier, Paul Oskar Kristeller, and John Herman Randall, Jr. (Chicago, 1948), pp. 36-46.
31. Giovanni di Pagolo Morelli, *Ricordi*, ed. Vittore Brance (Florence, 1969), pp. 300-01: "Fuggi quanto puoi maninconia o pensiero . . . Se hai cavallo, vatti a sollazzo per la terra e di fuori la mattina pello fresco e la sera."
32. *I libri della famiglia*, ed. Cecil Grayson (Scrittori d'Italia, 21; Bari, 1960), pp. 198-99.
33. The text in English translation may be found in *The Portable Medieval Reader*, ed. James Bruce Ross and Mary Martin McLaughlin (New York, 1949), pp. 517-18.
34. *I Fioretti de San Francesco*, ed. Guido-Davico Bonino (Turin, 1964), p. 100, cap. 21.

CHAPTER 8: GLICK

1. "Rats," *Quarterly Review* 201 (1857); 128, following *A Treatise on the Rat*, by "Uncle James" (1850).
2. A *stable* urban ecosystem is probably a contradiction in terms. The best one can hope for is a *stabilized* or *controlled* system in which the most harmful aspects of instability are minimized by technological and organizational means. See Richard L. Meier, "A Stable Urban Ecosystem: Its Evolution within Densely Populated Societies," *Habitat* 2 (1977); 173-88.
3. It is generally admitted that London reached its pre-Plague size again around 1377, although estimates of what that size may have been vary from thirty to sixty thousand.
4. R. E. Butler, "The Buried Rivers of London," *London Naturalist*, 41 (1962); 31-41.
5. Ernest L. Sabine, "Latrines and Cesspools of Mediaeval London," *Speculum* 9 (1934); 309-10; A. H. Thomas, ed., *Calendars of Plea and Memoranda Rolls, Preserved among the Archives of the City of London* (Cambridge, 1926), 4:152.
6. *Stow's Survey of London* (New York, 1965), p. 15; Butler, "Buried Rivers," pp. 31-32.
7. Thomas, *Calendars*, 2:93, 156-57; H. T. Riley, ed., *Memorials of London and London Life* (London: Longmans, 1868), pp. 295-96.

8. Gwyn A. Williams, *Medieval London. From Commune to Capital* (London: Athlone Press, 1963), pp. 84-85.
9. "Report of the Commissioners on the Chemical Quality of the Supply of Water to the Metropolis" (1851), *British Parliamentary Papers, Urban Areas, Water Supply* (9 vols.; Shannon: Irish University Press, 1968-70), 8:7-9 (original pagination).
10. *Ibid.*, p. 9.
11. "Metropolis Water Bill 1851," *British Parliamentary Papers, Urban Areas, Water Supply,* 2:230, 232, 238-39.
12. *Ibid.*, p. 239.
13. "Metropolis Water Supply Bills, 1852," *British Parliamentary Papers, Urban Areas, Water Supply,* 3:97.
14. "Report of Henry Letheby on Chemical and Sanitary Inquiries into the Matter of the Main Drainage of the Metropolis" (March 15, 1858), *British Parliamentary Papers, Urban Areas, Sanitation* (7 vols.; Shannon, 1969-70), 4:71-72, 74.
15. *The Lancet,* July 25, 1857, p. 91.
16. *Ibid.*, June 26, 1858, p. 632.
17. *Ibid.*, July 10, 1858, p. 41: "The Thames." Zymosis was a contagious disease ostensibly caused by fermentation.
18. *Punch,* July 31, 1858, p. 48: "Science and Smell;" see Stanley Hyland, *Curiosities from Parliament* (London, 1955), p. 72.
19. *Life and Letters of Faraday,* ed. Bence Jones, (2 vols.; London: Longmans, Green, 1870), 2:363-64 (July 7, 1855).
20. *Punch,* July 17, 1858, p. 22: "Committee on the Thames."
21. *The Lancet,* July 2, 1859, p. 19: "The Thames." The summer of 1859 was a repeat of that of 1858; the stench was countered by deodorization. The total quantity of disinfecting agents poured into the river that summer amounted to 4,281 tons of carbonic acid (*The Lancet,* October 8, 1859).
22. "Water Supply to the Metropolis and Large Towns, Report from the Royal Commission, 1868-69," *British Parliamentary Papers, Urban Areas, Water Supply,* 8:345 (May 8, 1869).
23. *Ibid.*, p. 431.
24. Derek J. DeSolla Price, "Is Technology Historically Independent of Science? A Study in Statistical Historiography," *Technology and Culture* 6 (1965); 568.
25. "Report on the Means of Deodorizing and Utilizing the Sewage of Towns" (1857), *British Parliamentary Papers, Urban Areas, Sanitation,* 4:4.
26. "Water Supply to the Metropolis and Large Towns," p. lxv.
27. *Times,* July 1, 1858.

CHAPTER 9: MONEYHON

1. *DeBow's Review* 5 (July 1868).
2. Alexis de Tocqueville, *Democracy in America,* quoted in Robert McHenry, ed., *A Documentary History of Conservation in America* (New York, 1972), pp. 117-18.
3. James Muirhead, *Land of Contrasts* (New York, 1902), p. 5.
4. Frederick Jackson Turner, *The Frontier in American History* (New York, 1920), pp. 266-67.
5. Simon Patten, *The New Basis of Civilization* (New York, 1907), p. 5.
6. Newton C. Blanchard, *Proceedings of a Conference of Governors in the White House* (Washington, D.C., 1909), p. 3.
7. W. J. McGee, "The Conservation of Natural Resources," *Proceedings of the Mississippi Valley Historical Association* 3 (1909-10); 371; see also Gifford Pinchot, *The Fight for Conservation* (Garden City, N.Y., 1910), pp. 40, 52, 109-10.

8. McGee, "Conservation of Natural Resources," pp. 365-67.
9. Charles R. Van Hise, *The Conservation of Natural Resources* (New York, 1910), p. 378.
10. John W. Powell, "Institutions for the Arid Lands," *The Century* (May 1890); see also John W. Powell, *Report on the Lands of the Arid Region of the United States* (Cambridge, Mass. 1962), pp. ix-xi.
11. John Muir, *The Yosemite* (New York, 1912), pp. 256-57; Charles W. Eliot, "The Need for Conserving the Beauty and Freedom of Nature in Modern Life," *The National Geographic Magazine* 26 (July 1914); 67-73; Frederick Law Olmsted, "The Yosemite Valley and the Marioposa Trees," *Landscape Architecture* 43 (1952); 20-21.
12. John Burroughs, *The Summit of the Years* (Boston, 1913), p. 50.
13. *Ibid.*, pp. 74-75.
14. George P. Marsh, *The Earth as Modified by Human Action* (New York, 1874), pp. iii, 54-55.
15. Nathaniel Shaler, *Man and the Earth* (New York, 1904), p. 231; Nathaniel Shaler, *Nature and Man in America* (New York, 1891), p. 283.
16. Liberty Hyde Bailey, *The Holy Earth* (New York, 1915), pp. 30-31; Edward Evans, "Ethical Relations between Man and Beast," *The Popular Science Monthly* 45 (September 1894); 634-46.
17. George L. Knapp, "The Other Side of Conservation," *North American Review* 191 (April 1910).
18. Quoted in McHenry, *A Documentary History of Conservation in America*, pp. 310-11.
19. Muir, *The Yosemite*, p. 262.

CHAPTER 10: CULBERTSON

1. The view taken here does not support either the doctrine of such eighteenth-century enthusiasts for "reason" as Bentham and Comte that religion and the wisdom of the past are to be banished as "superstition" or the claims of present-day proponents of omnipotent "science." On the contrary, we should characterize their simple, mechanistic—and implicitly providentialist—world as belonging to the new superstition. The view taken here would distinguish a domain of naturalistic knowledge that is needed to manage events in nature—from appendicitis operations to economies and ecological systems—from a domain of inspiration, religion, or intuitive values which must be invoked in final choices as to the goals of human life and human civilization, the way people usefully view themselves and their society, and the artistic values and style a society is to exemplify. What is criticized in this paper is ideology and pseudo-science masquerading as naturalistic knowledge, causing unrealistic world views and potentially catastrophic policies.
2. Address to Constituents, September 17, 1842, quoted in Brooks Adams, "The Heritage of Henry Adams," in Henry Adams, *The Degradation of Democratic Dogma* (1919; rept. New York, 1949), pp. 27-28.
3. Letter to Rev. Charles W. Upham, February 2, 1837, reprinted in *ibid.*, p. 25. Adams's references to Providence, we should perhaps note, do not imply a providentialist attitude toward policy. In his mind, while Providence may have provided the opportunity, man could make effective use of it only through positive government action based on knowledge, on applied science.
4. Adams's colorful characterization is evocative: "The thirst of a tiger for blood is the fittest emblem of the rapacity with which the members of all the new states fly at the public lands. The constituents upon whom they depend are all settlers, or tame and careless spectators of the pillage. They are themselves enormous speculators and land-jobbers." Quoted in *ibid.*, p. 31.

Index